PONTIFICAL INSTITUTE OF MEDIAEVAL STUDIES

SUBSIDIA MEDIAEVALIA

III

ASSART DATA AND LAND VALUES

TWO STUDIES IN THE EAST MIDLANDS 1200-1350

by

J. A. RAFTIS

PONTIFICAL INSTITUTE OF MEDIAEVAL STUDIES
TORONTO, CANADA
1974

ISBN 0-88844-352-8

PRINTED BY UNIVERSA, WETTEREN (BELGIUM)

to the

MEMORY

of

DAVID JOSLIN

late Professor of Economic History

University of Cambridge

TABLE OF CONTENTS

Preface	9
Study I. Land Values in the Inquisitions Post Mortem of the East Midlands to 1350	11
General Introduction	12
Arable	19
General Remarks on Table I	19
Summary	19
Value-Frequency	23
Table I	27
Meadow	49
General Remarks on Table II	49
Summary	50
Value-Frequency	51
Table II	55
Pasture	73
General Remarks on Table III	73
Summary	74
Value-Frequency	75
Table III	79
Wood	87
General Remarks on Table IV	87
Summary	88
Value-Frequency	89
Table IV	92
Study II. The End of Assarting in Some Royal Forests of the East Midlands	97
General Observations	98
Table I	101
Table II	108
Appendix I: Assarting in the Royal Forest of Northamptonshire in the Early Thirteenth Century	110

Table: Salcey Forest 111
Table: Whittlewood Forest 112
Table: Rockingham Forest 114
Appendix II: Mid Thirteenth Century Assart Data for Northamptonshire Forest 118
Table: Salcey Forest 120
Table: Whittlewood Forest 121
Table: Rockingham Forest 124
Appendix III: Northamptonshire Assarting in the Later Thirteenth Century 128
Table: Salcey Forest 128
Table: Whittlewood Forest 128
Table: Rockingham Forest 129
Appendix IV: Rent and Sowing of the Waste in the first half of the Fourteenth Century 131
Table A: Rent and Sowing of the Waste in Salcey and Whittlewood 132
Table B: Waste Rentals in the Rockingham Forest 133
Table C: Sowing of the Waste in Rockingham Forest 135
Appendix V: Assarts in the Royal Forests of Buckinghamshire in the Mid Thirteenth Century 138
Table A: First List; Second List; Third List; Fourth List; Fifth List 139
Table B: 1249-59 (34 H. III) 145
1252-53 (37 H. III) 146
1254-55 (39 H. III) 148
Table C: 1249-50. 1252-53. 1254-55 (Burnwood Forest only) 150
Appendix VI: Assarts in Huntingdonshire in the Thirteenth Century 151
Table A: Early Thirteenth Century 151
Table B: Mid Thirteenth Century 152
Table C: Assarts in Royal Forest of Huntingdonshire 1, July, 1286 152
Appendix VII: Early Thirteenth Century Assarts in Leicestershire and Rutland 154

Manuscripts Used Arranged in Chronological Order .. 156

Index of Places 157

PREFACE

Such is the extraordinary volume of many series of administrative records extant for mediaeval England that it has been necessary for various printed calendars of such series, and even editions of selected records, to omit common categories of data. The two series of records in question in the following study are the Forest Proceedings edited by G. J. Turner and the Calendar of Inquisitions Post Mortem produced by the Public Record Office. In the former, the many data upon the exact amounts of assarts were omitted; in the latter, manorial extents were not able to be printed. Complete editions of these materials would have required a score of volumes.

For a general study in the agrarian development of the East Midlands, this writer has found it necessary to extract these assarting and extent data. It is felt that these data are worth presenting in their own right, and some reasons for this are indicated in the following pages. Much more, however, it is thought that the tedious task of collecting such data need not be repeated for those interested in many more general questions as well as comparative problems of regional and local study. For this reason they are offered in this study. Other categories of data in these documents, above all numbers and size of waste in the Forest Proceedings and rents in the Inquisitions Post Mortem, have been omitted in part because these are not so readily comparable, but more because they would have required a study at least three times the size of this volume.

The very heavy labour involved in accumulating these data would have been impossible without the assistance of Miss Margaret Vowles who transcribed the Inquisitions over 1969-1970 and Miss Beryl Wells who identified many of the villages as well as setting up and typing the tables. I am also grateful to Canada Council for a short-term grant during the summer of 1971 to complete the research for this study.

STUDY I

LAND VALUES IN THE INQUISITIONS POST MORTEM OF THE EAST MIDLANDS TO 1350

Bibliographical Note:

The material for this study has been obtained from the manorial extents for the counties of Bedfordshire, Buckinghamshire, Hertfordshire, Huntingdonshire, Leicestershire, Northamptonshire, Nottinghamshire and Rutland. The file numbers of these extents were obtained from the *Calendar of Inquisitions Post Mortem*, volumes I-IX (1904-1917), Public Record Office, Chancery Records.

GENERAL INTRODUCTION

As a potential source for statistical data in mediaeval England the Inquisitions Post Mortem rank with Domesday Book and the Hundred Rolls and have indeed been widely employed by agrarian historians over the past one hundred years. And yet, unlike Domesday Book with its multitude of 'studies', the Inquisitions Post Mortem have never had their own historiographical tradition; nor, unlike the Hundred Rolls, even their own historian. Rather, the Inquisitions Post Mortem have suffered by comparison in the increasingly scientific analysis of other sources. The major strand of this current critical view may be traced to E. A. Kosminky's blunt statement: "It is certain, then, that we are dealing with an extremely unreliable source."[1] By the time of the English translation of Kosminsky's volume, his view concerning the Inquisitions Post Mortem was sufficiently widely held to be re-iterated by R. H. Hilton in a general review of sources with the explanation "... in many cases the jury gave evidence and escheators sent in returns that minimized the incomes and revenues of the estate."[2] Corroboration for Hilton's assessment may be found more recently in various quarters, for example, the criticism by C. D. Ross and T. B. Pugh of the Inquisitions Post Mortem as sources for the study of baronial income in the fifteenth century, and a similar criticism by J. C. Ward in her study of the income of the Clare family in the late thirteenth and early fourteenth centuries.[3]

However, the confused contemporary status of the Inquisitions is underlined by the fact that scholars do continue to employ

1 *Studies in the Agrarian History of England in the Thirteenth Cntury*, English tr. 1956, New York, p. 63.

2 "Sources of English Agrarian History", *The Agrarian History Review*, III, p. 14, 1955.

3 C. D. Ross and T. B. Pugh, "Materials for the Study of Baronial Incomes in Fifteenth-century England", *Ec. H. R.* 2nd series, vi, 186-8. J. C. Ward, *The Estates of the Clare Family*, 1066-1317, unpublished Ph. D. thesis, London, 1962.

these sources despite those absolute strictures indicated above. Perhaps somewhat illogically, Kosminsky follows the above-quoted remark with the qualifier: "On the other hand, a comparison of the figures they contain, carried out over wide areas, enables us to capture certain characteristic traits, certain peculiarities which, though vague, are vital."[4] And he did in fact study more than four hundred manorial surveys attached to the Inquisitions of the time of Henry III and early Edward I. The experience of other scholars has been more positive. For example, Dr. I. S. W. Blanchard, in his important study of economic change in Derbyshire in the late Middle Ages, uses Inquisitions Post Mortem very effectively.[5] Dr. P. F. Brandon, in his thorough analysis of mediaeval clearances in the East Sussex Weald, states concerning an extent to be found in an Inquisition Post Mortem of 1265: "There is nothing in the rentals and minister's accounts of Rotherfield Manor to suggest that the details of this extent are not essentially accurate."[6]

This sort of evidence cautions one against the total neglect of the Inquisitions Post Mortem. But one's suspicions about any neglect of the Inquisitions are more thoroughly aroused by the important position of these Inquisitions in a highly refined system of government administration. The *Guide to Contents of the Public Record Office*[7] describes these documents in the following fashion: "Inquisitions Post Mortem are inquests held, on the death of any tenant supposed to hold of the King in chief, by the escheator or escheators of the several counties or district, who either in obedience to writ of *diem clausit extremum* or merely in virtue of their office summoned a jury to inquire upon oath of what lands, etc., the tenant was seised at the time of his death, by what rents or services they were held, and the name and age of the next heir, in order that the king might be duly informed of his right of escheat or wardship or other advantages accruing to him". V. H. Galbraith cited these inquests as part of the regular operation of government involving "... co-operation between the two departments of Chancery and Exchequer by Chancery practice of making duplicates of the Inquisitions Post Mortem or

4 *Ibid.*, p. 63.

5 Ph. D. thesis, London, 1967.

6 "Mediaeval Clearances in the East Sussex Weald", note 19, p. 150, *Transactions of the Institute of British Geography*, 1969, and further his unpublished thesis as indicated in the same note.

7 I, 1963, p. 27.

inquiries into the land held by a tenant in chief at his death, the duplicates being forwarded to the Exchequer."[8] The fullest treatment of the Inquisitions Post Mortem, in equally positive terms, is to be found in the chapter on "The Escheator", by E. R. Stevenson in *The English Government at Work 1326-36.*[9] Surely this vast machinery of Angevin government, that had the initiative to juggle with a half-dozen varieties of assessment for taxation over the late thirteenth and early fourteenth centuries, could not have remained blind to those thousands of extents over several generations being 'extremely unreliable sources', if such were indeed the case!

Undoubtedly much more light will be thrown on the Inquisitions Post Mortem by the historians of government. There is, for example, an original study on wardship now in its final stages of preparation for the press that will fill out one area of the escheators role.[10] But for the purposes of this essay it will be enough to recall the long-recognized fact that these Inquisitions were of three types. By far the greater number of inquests indicated simply the facts of tenure, amounts and location of the property without detailing the items of income that are to be found in those inquests accompanied by extents.[11] Furthermore, even among the extents, many are merely sums of moneys accruing to various fees or proportions of fees, without details of the origins of the moneys. It is only those fuller extents, as the Calendars usually describe them,[12] that usually give information under about a dozen headings.[13]

8 P. 43, *The Public Records*, Oxford, 1934, and see further, Sir Maurice Powicke, *King Henry III and the Lord Edward*, i, 105-8.

9 II, ed. W. A. Morris & J. R. Strayer, Cambridge, Mass. 1942.

10 Sue Sheridan Walker, *Royal Wardship in Medieval England*, unpublished Ph. D. thesis, University of Chicago, 1966.

11 Cf. Stevenson, *op. cit.*, p. 135.

12 A student of the Inquisitions Post Mortem cannot fail to express his gratitude for the *Calendars* published by the Stationery Office, and the ease of accessibility of the manuscripts through the indication of file and number of documents in the file.

13 Cf. Kosminsky, *op. cit.*, pp. 47-48: "VALUATION OF DEMESNE: 1. Estimated value of homestead, court, garden, vineyard, dovecote, etc.; 2. Area of arable land, and its estimated value; 3. Area of meadow land in acres, and estimated value; 4. Area of pasture land, and estimated value; 5. Area of woodland, and its estimated value, often with an indication of the different items of revenue from this source; 6. List of mills, and their estimated annual revenue; 7. Secondary sources of income: salt-pans, peat, fisheries, ovens, breweries, etc.

Valuation of holdings: 1. The money rent (*redditus assisae*) of free holdings; 2. The money rent of villein holdings; 3. The labour dues of villeins and their equivalent in

Fortunately, historians of the agrarian economy of mediaeval England have not sought for the same sort of thoroughness and 'reliability' in manorial extents, inquisitions, surveys, account rolls and land charters that Kosminsky looked for in the Inquisitions Post Mortem. The economic historian accustomed to the completeness of modern accounting has had to bear two things in mind when dealing with the former type of record. First, those records of value (*valors*) and *a fortiori* of profits, do not relate all revenues since a goodly number are taken for granted; secondly, the more commonly extant surveys and account rolls do not provide a total inventory — again, many basic units of land and equipment are taken for granted. As a consequence, rather than attempting statistical assessments of more total productive units such as family estates, villages, manors or demesnes, statistical tabulation heretofore undertaken has tended to turn about single elements of revenue, above all quantities and prices of primary units of land, corn, livestock and labour supposedly sufficiently uniform for comparison.[14] Difficulties with the size of the bushel have shown scholars how treacherous even this elementary tabulation may be.[15] And possibly more variations, for example in the size of the customary acre, may have to be taken into account in the future. But in the meantime comparison of such simple aggregates can be a useful point of departure.

The most thorough study of accounting in mediaeval agrarian England does indeed now place the Inquisitions Post Mortem in the same context as manorial administration.[16] If this more modest comparative approach be taken to the Inquisitions Post

money (often only a money assessment of these dues is given); 4. Produce rent, sometimes valued in money terms; 5. Revenues of the manor court (*placita et perquisita*); 6. Estimate of revenue from view of frank-pledge, market, trading dues, the hundred-court."

14 The classical studies of the hide, etc. in Domesday studies, as well as the histories of prices from Rogers through Beveridge, and the tabulation from manorial accounts as in my *Estates of Ramsey Abbey*, have only been possible by comparative use of data.

15 Cf. J. Z. Titow, "Land and Population on the Bishop of Winchester's Estates, 1209-1350", unpublished Ph. D. thesis, Cambridge, 1962. In part, this is now published as *Winchester Yields: a study in medieval agricultural productivity*, Cambridge, 1972.

16 Dorothea Oschinsky, *Walter of Henley and other treatises on estate management and accounting*, Oxford, *1971*, p. 69: "The extents which were incorporated in the *Inquisitiones post mortem* — from 39 Henry III — follow the same pattern and, similarly, give the value of the estates in every detail." ... "By value was then understood the annual income from the estate not its capital value; as one copyist of *Walter* commented 'the land is yours and is not reckoned' (*Walter* app. c.61)."

Mortem may it not be possible to avoid the rather moralistic deductions of Kosminsky about the 'unreality' (p. 48, 57) or 'carelessness' (p. 60) of these records? For Kosminsky has of course well established that many items are consistently omitted from the Inquisition.[17] But the corollary, that many items are consistently required for the extents in Inquisitions Post Mortem, may still be of significance. The purpose of this essay is to trace the findings of such a procedure for eight counties of the East Midlands.

In comparison with other sources for agrarian history in the thirteenth century,[18] perhaps the most unique feature of the Inquisitions Post Mortem are the acreage evaluations. Of the wide variety of data available in these Inquisitions, therefore, the following study is only concerned with acre evaluations. The acre is also the most widely employed unit in the Inquisitions Post Mortem, and therefore, the most suitable for comparison. It is known of course that the customary acre might vary in size from one part of the county to another, as in some forest villages of Northamptonshire,[19] for example, where the acre was larger than the average throughout the Midlands. But for the geographical region under concern here, and the chronological period, it seems to be an acceptable assumption that the size of the acre did not change. Therefore, while it is only a hypothesis of the following study that the acre was about the same size throughout the East Midlands, it is more strongly felt that for chronological comparisons of changes in value in one village the acre may be taken to have been the same size in 1340 as in 1280.

Clearly, of course, these figures do not represent gross measurements of revenue from arable, for even the areas of poorest corn yield would return more than the acreage values cited here. Nor is it obvious how the figure is derived as a measurement for net revenue since ordinary allocations from corn seem to be assumed. As will be illustrated more fully below, indications of the latter are given by the terms *reprise*, 'above rent' and especially with the failure to evaluate fallow when it is in common pasture. Furthermore, there is no indication that the value

17 *Op. cit.*, pp. 57-58.

18 Such traditional tabulations as those by Rogers and Beveridge, for example, largely drawn from manorial accounts, do not deal with acre valuations at all.

19 That these variations were well known at the time is clear from treatises on accounting. Cf. model accounts edited in Oschinsky, *op. cit.*

of the acre relates to the particular crop sown in the rotation course of the year of the extent. Rather, one must assume that the evaluation pertains to an average type of grain (and corn price) over several years. And indeed the phrases of the extent, by referring to various sowings ('when sown', 'two-thirds sown', etc.) do imply such an average. However, notwithstanding this 'negative' nature of our information, unmistakably the acreage entries are employed to designate real values of acres sown, and therefore must be taken on their own terms as meaningful measures of arable values.

Further indication of the average value, rather than total, is given in the different methods of reporting acres sown over the three generations and more of the Inquisitions under consideration here. Until late in the time of Edward II the inquisitors simply state that a certain number of acres are worth so much per acre, and the totals of the extent show that all the acres reported are taken as sown.[20] From the 1320's for many properties there is given the proportion of the total arable sown in the rotation of any year. Again, the values are stated to be for these sown acres only. For example, for Huntingdonshire the first reference to numbers of acres actually sown per year is 17 Ed II, for Rutland in 18 Ed II there is a first reference to two parts sown, in Hertfordshire a new type of reference is given in 18 Ed II when acres are evaluated as sown or not sown.

For the following tables, therefore, the presentation is simply of numbers of acres indicated in the extent in the first column for each village, followed by the valuation given for such acres and (in brackets) the regnal year of the extent. In order to depict changes over time, entries for each village are presented in these 'generations' — from the first entries in the Inquisitions Post Mortem to 25 Ed I, from 26 Ed I to end of Ed II, and from beginning of Ed III to approximately 1350. For convenience in tabulation acreage totals are rounded to the nearest figure. While for most entries the same manor is in question for extents over the several generations, this is obviously not always the case. However, for this study it has not been possible to trace estate histories of all entries in the Inquisition Post Mortem, so that the

20 E.g., in Rutland, for Barrowden three fields of 6 acres, 61 acres and 75 acres were noted to be worth 5d. per acre in 26 Ed I, and the total value clearly includes all these acres.

properties are no more than the tables indicate, that is of such and such village. Finally, since there is only rarely a correlation of meadow, pasture and wood values with those of arable, whereas common evaluation patterns run through these various elements throughout the whole East Midlands region, it has been found more useful to present arable, meadow, pasture and wood in separate tables.

Despite the unique features of this record for chronological comparison, in contrast with the regular national surveys such as the subsidy assessments, the surviving extents from the Inquisitions Post Mortem are a haphazard collection predicated upon accidents of death and geography. In order to provide a backdrop for data from these Inquisitions, therefore, these are analyzed against the study of the lay subsidy around the close of the second generation (1334) by B. E. Glasscock,[21] and the one-ninth assessment of 1341 by Alan R. H. Baker.[22]

21 R. E. Glasscock, "The Distribution of Wealth in East Anglia in the Early Fourteenth Century", *Transactions and Papers, The Institute of British Geographers*, no. 32 (1963), 113-123. And especially his unpublished Ph. D. thesis, London, 1962, "The Distribution of Lay Wealth in South-East England in the Early Fourteenth Century".

22 R. H. Baker, "Evidence in the 'Nonarum Inquisitiones' of Contracting Arable Lands in England during the Early Fourteenth Century", *Ec. H. R.* (1966), 2nd series, 19, 518-531.

ARABLE

GENERAL REMARKS ON TABLE I

The total number of entries (1343) reported for arable in Table I, embracing 213,870 acres, represents of course much more than meadow, pasture and wood taken together. As synopsized in the following lists, these data break down into three large acreage counties (Bucks, Northants, Herts), one medium-sized (Beds), three relatively small acreage totals (Hunts, Notts, Leicestershire), and the very small acreage for the county of Rutland. Something of the comparative potential of these data is given by a further breakdown according to generations:

TABLE I *SUMMARY*

	ENTRIES				ACREAGE			
		Generation				Generation		
County	1st	2nd	3rd	Total	1st	2nd	3rd	Total
Bedford	58	64	75	197	1049	9882	9184	29556
Bucks	85	117	95	297	14423	19942½	13429½	47795
Herts	51	80	49	179	13985½	17502	9370	40855
Hunts	24	29	26	79	5995	3681	3061	12692
Leics	16	68	33	117	3898	8110	4053½	16061½
Northants	83	136	115	334	14111	17566½	15797	47474½
Notts	47	25	37	109	6877	3203	3847	13887
Rutland	2	15	14	31	496½	2069	2983	5549
	Grand Total 1343				Grand Total 213,870			

The first impression is one of similar valuations running throughout the greater part of the East Midlands. Since common evaluations seem to be employed, however, when variations do occur among these more uniform data, the fall in value from 6 to 4 or 5 to 3 pence per acre ought very likely to be taken as significant marginal variations of 33% or 40% rather than slight shifts in total valuations. There is some evidence as to what these more total evaluations might have been. A unique entry indicates the actual standing crop as the valuation base.

The 60 acres at 'Chellington, Wymington and Risely' of Beds were evaluated at 48 pence per acre, apparently on the basis of the actual crops of wheat and rye growing on the arable at that time. It must also be suggested that the acre evaluations between 10 and 20 pence, occurring for the most part in the thirteenth century, are also to be explained by a different system of evaluation. By contrast with other manors in somewhat similiar geographical circumstances, these would seem to be more complete or actual market acre valuations for that year. That is to say, these higher values indicate more immediate or direct leasing rather than the more general farm values of the whole manor, for in most instances the higher values are associated with valuation according to the smaller units (especially virgates) rather than the largest (hide or oxgang).

In Rutland, where Oakham was valued at 20 pence to the acre, Market Overton at 10 pence and Langham at 12 pence against the average 6 pence, these higher values are associated with the lands being in the 'hands of bondsmen and free tenants'. Small units of exceptional value in other counties seem to be similarly evaluated, as with Pickwell, Leics (16), and in Northants, Torpel (12), Wicken (10) and Little Weldon (12). The virgate units were also given for Foston (17) in Leicestershire. The Inquisitions Post Mortem of the thirteenth century do not usually note the amount of the total arable actually sown in the year of the extent, but where this is done it would seem to explain some higher values. Such were Balderton (12) and Carlton in Lindrick (12) in Notts. In other instances a sharp change in valuation for some villages over a few years at this earlier period would seem to indicate that the higher evaluation was only for the acreage sown that year. Such variations occurred at Kimbolton (81/2, 4) in Hunts, Saddington in Leics (8, 31/2), at Laxton, Notts (10, 6), at Newbottle (12, 4) and Pilton (12, 7) in Northants, and in Bucks at Datchet (12, 6), Edlesborough (12, 6), Hardwick (12, 6) (10, 4, 8), Stoke Poges (3rd gen. 18, 8, 6, 4) and Weston (10, 4).

Other higher valuations for which there are no obvious explanations are not many: Normanton (12), Bottesford (12) and Donington (12) in Leics, in Northants, Easton (18), Cotterstock (12), Billing (12), Ecton (10), Halse (12), Long Buckby (12), and in Bucks at Cublington (11) and Seabrook (12). In Beds only Stanbridge (10) seems exceptional, but without explanation. The highest value in Herts, that of Sawbridgeworth (8) seems simply indicative of more valuable arable as do Washingley (8) and Diddington (8) in Hunts.

Taking the remaining range of values as more comparable, the Inquisitions Post Mortem data for the first half of our period confirm to a remarkable degree the regional analysis of wealth from the assessment for the subsidy of 1334.[1] Rutland, 'even' and 'wealthy' in the subsidy, is also in the following table fairly consistent and higher than the average acreage evaluation throughout the East Midlands. The arable of Hertfordshire and Leicestershire, in general less valuable in the subsidy assessment than Rutland, has this lower medium value well represented by the frequency of 4d values in the Inquisitions. While it is more difficult to speak of the remaining counties in general terms because of their great internal geographical diversities, in these counties too the most persistent values of clayland are 4d, frequently moving upward to 6d under better conditions. This is especially true for Bedfordshire, much better represented in the Inquisitions Post Mortem than Huntingdonshire. Consistently, too, the richer valley estates average around 8d to the acre. At the opposite pole, the poor upland soil, especially in the more lately cleared forested regions, was often worth only 2 or 3d to the acre. In these cases the valuation differential is more striking than those of the subsidy evaluation where such lands were only one-half or slightly less than one-half of the value of the wealthy zones in the region. The following table summarizes the frequency of various arable values.

Again, if one takes Rutland the smallest and most uniform county as the simplest model for a point of departure, the range of property values in the third generation does not seem to have changed much from the thirteenth century. These wealthy estates were able to maintain arable values. In Beds, on the other hand, the picture is that of a general decline in values of arable, especially after the second generation. For Leicestershire comparative data are not very many. Some of the more valuable properties, such as Ashby de la Zouch and Evington were maintained. But as far as the comparative evidence goes the picture is one of decline (Mowsley, Claybrook, Newbold, Hinckley, Earl Shilton, Desford, Bottesford, Branston, Groby). Increases were reported for Lowesby and Saddington. Where no comparative data are available, it may only be pointed out that lower values tend to concentrate more in the time of Edward III.

Comparative data for Herts are few for the first and third generations, so while it may be noted that there were many low values in the third period, some of these were already low by the

1 Cf. references above to the work of Glasscock.

second, and there was also a tendency for values to stabilise around the medium low unit. For Notts the comparative data are not great in number, although where these do exist there is fair evidence for clear fall in value by the third generation. There is also evidence for a considerable maintenance of values, and in general a picture of many small values in the third generation. These three features also appear in the evidence for Hunts, that is, a tendency towards smaller values in the third generation, where comparative values are available a predominance of decline in value, yet some evidence for stabilisation. In the great amount of data available for Northants there is good evidence for the many small values in the third generation, although also for maintenance on more valuable estates. In the very varied data for Bucks there is also a predominance of concentration about lower values in the third period, and a good comparative picture of the actual decline over the total period. But there is also interesting evidence for stability both about fairly low levels as well as higher levels of arable values.

In general, therefore, these Inquisitions Post Mortem data do substantiate other studies indicating a drastic decline in property values over the first half of the fourteenth century, especially for poorer lands where investment in capital could not be sustained.[1] However, these data also support studies of retrenchment, reorganization and stability for more wealthy estates (Britnell, Titow, etc.). Since the following table cannot indicate sowing on comparable land over the three generations, and there is much more detail about rotational sowing in the time of Edward the III than earlier, it would be hazardous to draw precise conclusions about actual decline in numbers of acres sown. That is to say, for the third generation there is frequently noted (in brackets in the table) the actual acres sown that year, and occasionally further information about value of the fallow as pasture. This is evidence for an advance in accounting procedure, but not very likely for a change in actual agrarian management since the thirteenth century.

1 Cf. the reference above to the article by A. R. H. Baker.

TABLE I *VALUE — FREQUENCY*

ARABLE

BEDFORDSHIRE

1st Generation

Values:	2	2½	3	3½	4	5	6	8	9	10	48
Frequency:	2	1	4	2	18	1	14	6	3	1	2

2nd Generation

Values:	3	4	6	7	8
Frequency:	11	38	13	1	1

3rd Generation

Values:	½	1	1½	2	3	4	5	6	8
Frequency:	1	1	1	11	12	1	2	6	1

BUCKINGHAMSHIRE

1st Generation

Values:	1	2	3	3½	4	5	6	8	9	10	11	12
Frequency:	1	2	7	1	25	3	29	7	1	2	1	4

2nd Generation

Values:	1	2	3	4	6	7	7½	8	9	10	12
Frequency:	4	13	16	46	25	1	1	2	3	2	3

3rd Generation

Values:	1	2	3	3½	4	5	6	7	8	18
Frequency:	2	11	21	1	40	2	11	1	1	1

VALUE — FREQUENCY

TABLE I cont'd

ARABLE

HERTFORDSHIRE

1st Generation

Values:	2	3	4	5	6	8
Frequency:	3	11	30	1	6	2

2nd Generation

Values:	2	2½	3	3½	4	5	6
Frequency:	9	2	31	1	31	2	5

3rd Generation

Values:	2	2½	3	4	6
Frequency:	14	2	11	26	2

HUNTINGDONSHIRE

1st Generation

Values:	1½	2½	4	6	8	8½
Frequency:	1	1	7	10	3	1

2nd Generation

Values:	2	3	4	6
Frequency:	4	6	13	6

3rd Generation

Values:	2	2½	3	4	5	6	7	16
Frequency:	2	1	4	12	3	2	1	1

VALUE — FREQUENCY

TABLE I cont'd

ARABLE

LEICESTERSHIRE

1st Generation

Values:	4	5	6	8	12
Frequency:	5	1	8	1	1

2nd Generation

Values:	2	3	3 1/2	4	5	6	8	9	12	16	17
Frequency:	7	9	1	29	2	13	2	1	2	1	1

3rd Generation

Values:	1	2	3	4	6	30s.	60s.
Frequency:	1	3	2	19	7	1	1

NOTTINGHAMSHIRE

1st Generation

Values:	3	4	5	5 1/2	6	6 1/2	7	8	9	10	12	20	1
Frequency:	3	17	1	2	14	1	2	2	1	1	2	1	1

2nd Generation

Values:	3	4	6
Frequency:	4	14	8

3rd Generation

Values:	1	2	3	4	5	6	12
Frequency:	1	7	4	9	1	12	1

VALUE — FREQUENCY

TABLE I cont'd

ARABLE

NORTHAMPTONSHIRE

1st Generation

Values:	2	3	4	5	6	7	8	9	10	12	18
Frequency:	1	2	13	5	40	2	6	4	3	8	1

2nd Generation

Values:	1	2	3	3½	4	5	6	7	8	9	10	12
Frequency:	1	5	16	2	48	7	42	1	7	2	4	2

3rd Generation

Values:	2	2½	3	3¼	3½	4	6	8	10	12	80
Frequency:	8	2	21	1	1	47	27	4	1	3	1

RUTLAND

1st Generation

Values:	3	4
Frequency:	1	1

2nd Generation

Values:	3	4	5	6	20
Frequency:	1	8	1	7	1

3rd Generation

Values:	2	3	4	6	10	12	20
Frequency:	1	1	4	4	1	2	1

TABLE I — *ARABLE*

	1st Gen.		2nd Gen.		3rd Gen.	
BEDFORDSHIRE						
Warden	212½	4 (1254)	40	4 (32 Ed I)	20 (½)	4 (7 Ed III)
(Gravenhurst)			13	4 (32 Ed I)		
Warden	60	4 (1280)			37½ (½)	4 (9 Ed III)
	54½	4 (1281)	—		—	
Wilden & Bolnhurst	(100)	6 (1264)	27	3 (11 Ed II)	48	5 (5 Ed III)
Wilden	144	8 (1269)	160	4 (15 Ed II)	18½	4 (23Ed III)
	80	8 (1270)	—		—	
Stevington	440	6 (1264)	—		180	4 (23 Ed III)
					20	3 (23 Ed III)
Radwell	180	4 (1266)	—		—	
Wrestlingworth	129	9 (1271)	132	6 (3 Ed II)	40	4 (11 Ed III)
					88 (½)	4 (15 Ed III)
					60 (½)	4 (15 Ed III)
Wreste Park			120	4 (1 Ed II)	—	
Cainhoe	300 (360?)	4 (1273)	80	3 (4 Ed II)	24	3 (20 Ed III)
	100	4 (15 Ed I)	80	3 (12 Ed II)	4	5 (20 Ed III)
			40	4 (18 Ed II)	73 (⅔)	2 (24 Ed III)
			40	4 (19 Ed II)	80	4 (23 Ed III)
					73 (⅔)	2 (24 Ed III)
					37 (⅔)	2 (24 Ed III)
Bromham	111	3½ (1278)	—		—	
	60	3½ (1286)				
(Chellington)	60 (Wheat)	48 (1282)				
(Wymington)	8 (Rye)	48 (1282)				
(Risely)						
Stagsden	330	4 (1283)	80	4 (4 Ed II)	81 (½)	4 (8 Ed III)
					211 (⅔)	2 (20 Ed III)
Eyworth	100	9 (1282)			200 (½)	4 (8 Ed III)
	110	9 (1284)				
Wymington	120	4 (1284)	240	4 (26 Ed I)	90 (½)	4 (21 Ed III)
					248	½d (25 Ed III)
					248 (⅔)	1½d (23 Ed III)
Millbrook	530	4 (1285)	120	4 (4 Ed II)	400 (240)	2 (4 Ed III)
					(160)	1 (4 Ed III)
Cotes (Eastcott)	600	6 (1285)	170	4 (4 Ed II)	60	6 (17 Ed III)
					300 (½)	4 (17 Ed III)
					or	2
Renhale	160	6 (1286)	140	6 (30 Ed I)		
			110	4 (8 Ed II)		
Dilwick (Stagsden)	357½	4 (1286)	357	4 (30 Ed I)	210	3 (9 Ed III)
Cardington	160	4 (1286)	140	4 (30 Ed I)		
			207	4 (11 Ed II)		
Keysoe	369	4 (23 Ed I)	80	4 (9 Ed II?)		
	349	4 (23 Ed I)	250	3 (17 Ed II)		
	349	4 (24 Ed I)				
Moggerhanger	176	4 (17 Ed I)				
Kempston	360	6 (18 Ed I)			240	4 (22 Ed III)
Chanston (Roxton)	200	6 (18 Ed I)	160	6 (30 Ed I)		
			40	4 (5 Ed II)		

	1st Gen.		2nd Gen.		3rd Gen.	
Astwick	136½	3 (19 Ed I)				
Stanbridge	170	10 (20 Ed I)				
	92 (48) or (44)	8 (1259)				
Shelton	350	6 (20 Ed I)				
Staploe	56	8 (20 Ed I)				
Sutton	149½	6 (20 Ed I)			200 (⅔)	3 (9 Ed III)
					20 + 38	4 (23 Ed III)
					8	1 (24 Ed III)
Eaton (Bray)	134	8 (22 Ed I)				
	327	8 (1274)	321	4 (27 Ed I)		
Sandy	287½	2½ (22 Ed I)				
Tempsford	17½	6 (22 Ed I)				
	7	6 (22 Ed I)				
	2	6 (22 Ed I)				
	9½	6 (22 Ed I)				
	6½	3 (22 Ed I)				
Aspley Guise	160	3 (23 Ed I)				
Wootton	400	6 (23 Ed I)	40	3 (17 Ed II)	46 (⅔)	4 (10 Ed III)
					40	3 (17 Ed III)
					120 (⅔)	4 (8 Ed III)
					55	4 (9 Ed III)
					55	4 (10 Ed III)
(La) Hyde	80	2 (24 Ed I)				
Flitwick	100½	2 (24 Ed I)				
Edworth	140	6 (25 Ed I)	130	6 (15 Ed II)		
Westoning	219½	3 (25 Ed I)	160	4 (15 Ed II)		
Campton	320	4 (25 Ed I)				
Houghton (Conquest)			300	4 (26 Ed I)		
Streatley			140	3 (29 Ed I)		
Higham Gobion			360	6 (29 Ed I)		
Biggleswade			20	4 (32 Ed I)		
Dunton (by Biggleswade)					120 (⅔)	4 (7 Ed III)
Ravensden			138	8 (32 Ed I)		
Greathampstede			83	4 (2 Ed II)		
Wootton Pillinge			100	4 (2 Ed II)		
Cople			45	6 (2 Ed II)		
Thurleigh			200	4 (1 Ed II)		
			(204)	4 (17 Ed II)		
Brogborough			180	4 (1 Ed II)		
Ampthill			80	3 (4 Ed II)	120	4 (23 Ed III)
Haynes			420	6 (5 Ed II)	300	4 (1 Ed III)
Stotfold			180	4 (5 Ed II)	160	4 (1 Ed III)
Willington			400	6 (5 Ed II)	400	4 (1 Ed III)
Bletsoe			300	4 (6 Ed II)		
Blunham			190	4 (6 Ed II)		
Wyboston			160	6 (10 Ed II)		
			120	4 (17 Ed II)		
Yelden	360	5 (11 Ed II)				
Northill	150	6 (18 Ed I)	140	6 (11 Ed II)		
Meppershall			180	4 (13 Ed II)	240	3 (5 Ed III)
Arlesey			160	4 (15 Ed II)	100	4 (5 Ed III)

	1st Gen.		2nd Gen.		3rd Gen.	
Harrold			420	3 (17 Ed II)		
Santon Barn			260	3 (17 Ed II)		
Podington			486	3 (17 Ed II)		
Dunton					140 (½)	6 (2 Ed III)
					120 (½)	4 (6 Ed III)
Dunton (Chambeley)					93	4 (2 Ed III)
Shillington					120 (66)	6 (6 Ed III)
Barton-in-the-Clay					80 (48)	6 (6 Ed III)
Toddington					110	4 (7 Ed III)
					160 (½)	4 (7 Ed III)
					and	3 (7 Ed III)
					148 (½)	
Sudbury					180	4 (7 Ed III)
					200 (⅔)	4 (8 Ed III)
					80	4 (22 Ed III)
Henlow					100	4 (8 Ed III)
Milton Ernest					90 (½)	4 (8 Ed III)
Kempston Hardwick					90 (½)	4 (8 Ed III)
Langford					200	4 (10 Ed III)
					200	4 (22 Ed III)
Sundon					490½	6 (12 Ed III)
					(253)	
Turvey					8	4 (14 Ed III)
					237 (136)	2 (20 Ed III)
					16	4 (21 Ed III)
Beeston					16 (⅔)	8 (16 Ed III)
Nares Gladly					20	2 (20 Ed III)
Hockliffe					68 (½)	3 (24 Ed III)
Flitton			75½	3 (17 Ed II)		
Luton	97½	6 (1279)	44	4 (32 Ed I)	40	2 (Ed III)
	39	4 (1279)	70	4 (32 Ed I)	40	2 20 Ed III)
			90	4 (11 Ed II)		
			98	4 (27 Ed I)	48	3 (2 Ed III)
			104	4 (34 Ed I)	143 (80)	4 (4 Ed III)
					(63½)	2 (4 Ed III)
			65	4 (2 Ed II)		
			48½	4 (8 Ed II)	160 (⅔)	2 (23 Ed III)
Wood Croft (Luton)	129	6 (16 Ed I)			80	3 (20 Ed III)
Odell	240	4 (24 Ed I)	29	6 (1 Ed II)	300	4 (10 Ed III)
					300	4 (22 Ed III)
Odell (Little)	260	7 (32 Ed I)				
	144	6 (32 Ed I)				
BUCKINGHAMSHIRE						
Datchet	150	12 (38 H III)			193	6 (6 Ed III)
	100	6 (24 Ed I)				
Medenham	280	5 (48 H III)	144	4 (19 Ed II)	140	3 (21 Ed III)
	150	4 (15 Ed I)				
Chesham	240	3½ (48 H III)	60	4 (6 Ed II)	20	3 (5 Ed III)
	93	3 (15 Ed I)	80	4 (4 Ed II)	100	3 (5 Ed III)
	140	4 (24 Ed I)				
Chesham Bois			80	3 (4? Ed II)	180	3 (13 Ed II)
Whitchurch	200	6 (48 H III)			80	4 (5 Ed III)
	120	6 (24 Ed I)				

TABLE I

	1st Gen.		2nd Gen.		3rd Gen.	
Linford	120	10 (51 H III)				
Little Linford			160	4 (30 Ed I)	123	4 (12 Ed III)
			140	4 (19 Ed II)		
Great Linford					210	3½ (12 Ed III)
Edlesborough	90	6 (54 H III)	80	3 (32 Ed I)	109	4 (8 Ed III)
	98	6 (21 Ed I)	40	4 (5 Ed II)	63	2 (9 Ed III)
	44	12 (24 Ed I)	61	3 (9 Ed II)	34	4 (21 Ed III)
	33	6 (24 Ed I)	80	4 (9 Ed II)	62	2 (21 Ed III)
	32	4 (24 Ed I)			80 (⅔)	4 (23 Ed III)
Aston Clinton	(260)	(9) (56 H III)	142 (82)	4 (13 Ed II)		
			(60)	1 (13 Ed II)		
Risborough	455	10 (56 H III)	465	7 (28 Ed I)		
Burnham & Eton	290	6 (? H III)				
Burnham					100	6 (1 Ed III)
Hitcham	324	6 (20 Ed I)	Hitcham	& Losmere	160	4 (12 Ed III)
Losmere	160	4 (20 Ed I)				
Newport Pagnell	240	4 (20 Ed I)			300	4 (12 Ed III)
	403	6 (19 Ed I)			200	2 (12 Ed III)
	100	3 (19 Ed I)				
Wavendon	200	3 (2? Ed I)			170 (½)	4 (7 Ed III)
Haversham	349½	8 (2 Ed I)	300	4 (34 Ed I)	100	4 (9 Ed III) (or pasture)
			?(3) 240	4 (19 Ed II)	130	4 (21 Ed III)
Leckhampstead	240 (pasture)	4 (7 Ed I)	24	4 (10 Ed II)		
Leckhampstead (Great)	410	6 (8 Ed I)	80	9 (32 Ed I)		
Wycombe	255½	2 (9 Ed I)			140	2 (5 Ed III)
					160	2 (23 Ed III)
Buckland	110	6 (11 Ed I)			240 (⅓?)	4 (8 Ed III)
Fulbrook	90	6 (12 Ed I)	72	4 (33 Ed I)	30	5 (20 Ed III)
	90	4 (13 Ed I)				
Cublington	394½	11 (12 Ed I)	300	6 (33 Ed I)	160	4 (20 Ed III)
Shabbington			700	6 (6 Ed II)		
Grove	7+60	4 (13 Ed I)	180	2 (15 Ed II)		
Hambleden			300	3 (12 Ed II)	340	3 (12 Ed III)
Grendon Underwood	144½	6 (25 Ed I)	120	4 (29 Ed I)	200 (½)	4 (7 Ed III)
			144	6 (32 Ed I)	120 (80)	4 (8 Ed III)
			100	4 (4 Ed II)		
			140	7½ (18 Ed II)		
Crafton	160	6 (14 Ed I)	80	6 (32 Ed I)		
	110	6 (20 Ed I)				
Little Missenden	115	6 (33 H III)				
Great Missenden	165	3 (18 Ed I)	120	4 (29 Ed I)	136	3 (6 Ed III)
	137	4 (20 Ed I)			75	2 (11 Ed III)
Aylesbury	84	6 (23 Ed I)			300 (⅔)	4 (12 Ed III)
	453	6 (25 Ed I)				
Hardwick	200	12 (23 Ed I)	124½	8 (3 Ed II)		
	200	6 (25 Ed I)	140	4 (4 Ed II)		
			200	10 (9 Ed II)		

TABLE I

	1st Gen.		2nd Gen.		3rd Gen.	
Sherington	160	6 (24 Ed I)	145	6 (29 Ed I)		
			42	4 (31 Ed I)		
Chearsley	155	4 (24 Ed I)	160	4 (18 Ed II)		
Little Brickhill	100	4 (24 Ed I)	100	2 (35 Ed I)		
			334	4 (? Ed II)		
Great Brickhill			140	4 (1 Ed II)		
Wendover	260	4 (24 Ed I)	250	4 (30 Ed I)		
			50	1 (13 Ed II)		
Wendover & Weston Turville					100	4 (5 Ed III)
Hanslope			1000	6 (26 Ed I)		
			1000	6 (9 Ed II)		
			1000 (800-9)	(9 Ed II)		
			(200-9)			
			500	4 (18 Ed II)		
Amersham	180	2 (25 Ed I)	219	4 (27 Ed I)	720	3 (10 Ed III)
	180	3 (25 Ed I)	50	4 (4 Ed II)	45?	2 (8 Ed III)
Iver			180	6 (32 Ed I)	120	4 (23 Ed III)
			200	4 (3 Ed II)		
Stoke Poges			60½	12 (32 Ed I)	130	18 (5 Ed III)
					105	8 (5 Ed III)
					160	6 (5 Ed III)
					27½	4 (5 Ed III)
Marsworth			60	6 (30 Ed I)		
			200	6 (35 Ed I)	15	Nil (9 Ed III)
			200	6 (4 Ed II)	40 (⅔)	3 (9 Ed III)
			34	6 (9 Ed II)		
			280	3 (12 Ed II)		
Adstock			120	6 (33 Ed I)	120 (⅔)	4 (10 Ed III)
Stoke Goldington			120	6 (33 Ed I)	120	4 (1 Ed III)
			180	6 (2 Ed II)	38	3 (23 Ed III)
			80	4 (5 Ed II)	34	3 (23 Ed III)
Ilmer			380	6 (34 Ed I)	140	6 (3 Ed III)
Stewkley			100	2 (35 Ed I)		
Easington			100	3 (35 Ed I)		
Great Marlow			300	4 (35 Ed I)		
Marlow			301	4 (8 Ed II)		
Addington			170	3 (1 Ed II)	180	6 (3 Ed III)
Weston (Turville?)			200	4 (2 Ed II)		
			194	10 (9 Ed II)		
Weston Turville					200	3 (23 Ed III)
Gayhurst			80	4 (2 Ed II)	200 (⅔)	3 (23 Ed III)
Farnham Royal			480	2 (3 Ed II)		
			280	2 (10 Ed II)		
Holmer Green			80	3 (4 Ed II)	80	2 (9 Ed III)
Emberton			12	4 (5 Ed II)	120	3 (5 Ed III)
					20	3 (5 Ed III)
					40	3 (5 Ed III)
Padbury	168	6 (32 H III)				
	200	6 (22 Ed I)				
Chalfont St. Giles					80	1 (23 Ed III)

TABLE I

		1st Gen.		2nd Gen.		3rd Gen.
Chalfont	186½	6 (32 H III)				
Fulmer	40	8 (38 H III)				
	80	4 (24 Ed I)				
Eakley Lanes	83	4 (? H III)				
Hillesden	213	4 (20 Ed I)				
Tyringham	204	8 (2 Ed I)				
Astwood	146	6 (2 Ed I)				
Pirney (Astwood)	15	8 (2 Ed I)				
Wing	140	1+ (3 Ed I)				
Linslade	120	3(or 4?) (3 Ed I?)				
Linslade & Southcott	60	4 (14 Ed I)				
Cheddington	31	8 (13? Ed I)				
Ellesborough	21 + 21	6 (16 Ed I)				
Boarstall	101	3 (17 Ed I)				
	60	3 (17 Ed I)				
Waddesdon	404	5 (20 Ed I)				
Seabrook	140	12 (21 Ed I)				
Drayton Beauchamp			100	4 (6 Ed II)		
Drayton Parslow	93½	4 (21 Ed I)				
Hartwell	60	8 (22 Ed I)				
	129	8 (23 Ed I)				
Hampden	36	4 (22 Ed I)				
	36	4 (23 Ed I)				
Oakley	230	4 (22 Ed I)				
Little Broughton by Aylesbury	292	6 (25 Ed I)			339	7 (23 Ed III)
Broughton					80 (2/3)	3 (23 Ed III)
Kingsey			160	6 (26 Ed I)		
Dunton			126½	3 (26 Ed I)		
			60	2 (16 Ed II)		
			30	1 (16 Ed II)		
Feldham			80	3 (27 Ed I)		
Pitstone			100	3 (32 Ed I)		
Woburn			(40)	3 (29 Ed I)		
			(21)	3 (29 Ed I)		
			(15)	3 (29 Ed I)		
			(9)	3 (29 Ed I)		
Wingrave			63	4 (29 Ed I)		
Olney			80	4 (30 Ed II)	180	4 (17 Ed III)
			12	6 (30 Ed II)		
Dorney			73	4 (33 Ed I)		
Buckingham			240	4 (33 Ed I)		
			80	4 (20 Ed II)		
La Waterhall			100	6 (1 Ed II)		
Eton			200	4 (1 Ed II)		
Stoke Hammond			80	6 (1 Ed II)		
			200	2 (17 Ed II)		
Snelson			200	4 (1 Ed II)		
Eythorpe			140	8 (2 Ed II)		
Eythorpe & Cranwell			96	4 (18 Ed II)		
Ickford			36	6 (6 Ed II)		
Saunderton			14	4 (6 Ed II)		

	1st Gen.		2nd Gen.		3rd Gen.	
Dinton			320	4 (7 Ed II)		
Worminghall			52	2 (8 Ed II)		
Lavendon			244	12 (9 Ed II)		
Chilton			272	12 (9 Ed II)		
Whelpley Hill (Chesham)			120	2 (15 Ed II)		
La Burrow & Parmoor (Hambleden)			140	2 (17 Ed II)		
Woughton-on-the-Green			30	3 (17 Ed II)		
Beachendon			180	6 (18? Ed II)	180	4 (1 Ed III)
Stantonbury			120	6 (18 Ed II)		
			80	1 (18 Ed II)		
			40	4 (19 Ed II)		
			60	2 (19 Ed II)		
Hardmead			200	4 (19 Ed II)		
Penn			83	2 (19 Ed II)		
Whaddon	222	4 (25 Ed I)			254 (1/2)	4 (7 Ed III)
Singleborough	172	4 (25 Ed I)			100 (2/3)	4 (8 Ed III)
Aston Sanford					164	3 (2 Ed III)
Aston Bernard (Mullins)					304	6 (3 Ed III)
Calverton					90	4 (5 Ed III)
Gt. & Little Kimble					120	4 (5 Ed III)
					180	3 (23 Ed III)
					100	5 (5 Ed III)
Hoggeston					200	4 (23 Ed III)
(Gt. & Little)					24	4 (5 Ed III)
Horwood					80	3 (23 Ed III)
Woolstone					120	4 (7 Ed III)
(Gt. & Little)					5	6 (7 Ed III)
Foscott					180	(2/3) (7 Ed III)
					20	? (7 Ed III)
Bradenham					100	4 (7 Ed III)
Ashendon					200 (2/3)	4 (8 Ed III)
Westbury & Radclive					320	3 (9 Ed III)
Chenies (Isenhampsted)					200	4 1/2 (9 Ed III)
Preston Bisset					85	4 (12 Ed III)
					50	4 (17 Ed III)
Cowley					15	4 (12 Ed III)
Caldecote					40	3 (14 Ed III)
Caldecote & Willen					60	3 (14 Ed III)
Shenley					100 (2/3)	4 (15 Ed III)
Chivery in Aston Clinton					220 (1/2)	2 (15 Ed III)
Oak End					80 (1/2)	2 (15 Ed III)
Dorton (by Brehulle)					120 (2/3)	4 (17 Ed III)
Northall					40	4 (18 Ed III)
					40	2 (18 Ed III)

TABLE I

	1st Gen.		2nd Gen.		3rd Gen.	
Salden					150 (2/3)	6 (23 Ed III)
					(1/3)	3 (23 Ed III)
					300 (2/3)	6 (23 Ed III)
					300	6 (5 Ed III)
Milton Keynes					400 (2/3)	6 (23 Ed III)
					(1/3)	1 (23 Ed III)
Lathbury	100	4 (15 Ed I)	90	4 (4 Ed II)		
			100	4 (10 Ed II)		
Cippenham	318	6 (32 H III)	450	6 (28 Ed I)		
Weedon	50	6 (23 Ed I)	80	6 (4 Ed II)	200 (2/3)	4 (23 Ed III)
Wolverton	200	6 (32 H III)			200	4 (15 Ed III)
					200	3 (23 Ed III)
East Claydon	342	5 (25 Ed I)	192	3 (6 Ed II)		
	442	4 (25 Ed I)	288	3 (6 Ed II)		
			240	2 (3 Ed II)		
HERTFORDSHIRE						
Sacombe	360	4 (37 H III)	400	3 (8 Ed II)	190 (119)	4 (7 Ed III)
	320	4 (11 Ed I)	400	3 (14 Ed II)		
	160	3 (17 Ed I)				
Standon	253	6 (46? H III)	587	4 (35 Ed I)		
			240	3 (1 Ed II)	320	4 (15 Ed III)
	1076	5 (24 Ed I)	160	3 (8 Ed II)	291 (231)	(23 Ed III)
			700	3 (8 Ed II)		
Meesden	517½	6 (47 H III)	360	4 (7 Ed II)		
Albury	112	4 (47 H III)	100	4 (34 Ed I)		
	120	4 (55 H III)				
Flamstead	840	4 (48 H III)	80	3 (32 Ed I)	400	3 (11 Ed III)
			400	3 (3 Ed II)		
			300	3 (9 Ed II)		
Gt. Berkhamsted	400	4 (56 H III)	427	6 (32 Ed I)		
Little Berkhamsted	300	3 (23 Ed I)	360	6 (3 Ed II)	300 (200)	3 (11 Ed III)
			300	3 (9 Ed II)		
					16	4 (19 Ed III)
					or	2 (as past)
					(360)	2 (? Ed III)
Sawbridgeworth	517	8 (56 H III)	200	4 (4 Ed II)		
	200	8 (23 Ed I)	547	4 (15 Ed II)		
	330	6 (23 Ed I)				
Offley	21	3 (6 Ed I)	120	4 (2 Ed II)	150 (100)	4 (9 Ed III)
	200	4 (20 Ed I)	320 (96)	4 (20 Ed II)	360 160	4 (9 Ed III)
	100	2 (20 Ed I)	204	4 (20 Ed II)	200	2½
					200	4 (23 Ed III)
					(on past)	2
Walkern	519	4 (8 Ed I)	276	4 (6 Ed II)		
Gt. Wymondley	360	4 (11 Ed I)	240	4 (12 Ed II)		
Little Wymondley	89	4 (11? Ed I)	140	3 (12 Ed II)		
			100	3 (12 Ed II)		
Wyddial	540	6 (12 Ed I)			300 (200)	4 (15 Ed III)
					100	2 (15 Ed III)
					60	3 (15 Ed III)

		1st Gen.		2nd Gen.		3rd Gen.
Gaddesden	106	3 (12 Ed I)	105	4 (15 Ed I)		
	80	3 (20 Ed I)	123	3 (15 Ed I)		
Gt. Gaddesden			200	3 (7 Ed II)		
Little Gaddesden			80	4 (30 Ed I)	100	3 (20 Ed III)
			146	4 (33 Ed I)		3 (20 Ed III)
Wigginton	116	3 (12 Ed I)	160	2½ (33 Ed I)	120	4 (3 Ed III)
King's Walden	366	2 (14 Ed I)	400	6 (7 Ed II)	400	4 (3 Ed III)
	382	2 (14 Ed I)			100	
	61½	4 (6 Ed I)				
Little Hormead	164	4 (14 Ed I)	180	4 (7 Ed II)		
Hormead	560	4 (24 Ed I)	80	6 (7 Ed II)		
	132	4 (14 Ed I)	152	4 (4 Ed II)		
Rableyheath			80	4 (4 Ed II)	80	6 (9 Ed III)
Watton at Stone	330	4 (14 Ed I)	200	3 (16 Ed II)	280	3 (3 Ed III)
Pirton	200	4 (23 Ed I)	240	4 (33 Ed I)	132	4 (21 Ed III)
Theobald St. (Oldenham)	100	3 (24 Ed I)	80	2 (27 Ed I)		
Pope's Hall (Buckland)	147	6 (24 Ed I)	120	2 (8 Ed II)		
Eastwick			300	3 (29 Ed I)		
			392	5 (11 Ed II)		
			80	5 (11 Ed II)		
Eastwick atte Flore					380	4 (15 Ed III)
Bishops Hatfield			160	3 (32 Ed I)	60	2 (1 Ed III)
			300	4 (1 Ed II)	20	2 (1 Ed III)
			124	2 (18 Ed II)	15	2 (1 Ed III)
Gt. Bishey Wood (Wheathampstead)			120	2 (34 Ed I)		
Bishey Wood					314	3 (4 Ed III)
					239	2 (4 Ed III)
Abbots & Kings Langley			180	4 (32 Ed I)	133 2½	1½ (23 Ed III)
Batchwood (Childwickshay)			140	3 (2 Ed II)		
Hertingfordbury			360	3 (3 Ed II)		
			387	4 (18 Ed II)		
Gt. Anstey			240	4 (7 Ed II)		
Anstey					100	3 (15 Ed III)
Anstey (Little)			120	4 (7 Ed II)		
Westreed			60	4 (8 Ed II)		
Reed					100 (70)	4 (15 Ed III)
Stagenhoe			180	2 (9 Ed II?)		
Willian			80	3 (9 Ed II)	200	2 (23 Ed III)
Berwick			240	4 (12 Ed II)		
Shenley			120	3 (12 Ed II)		
Throcking			40	2 (12 Ed II)		
Hunsdon	160	4 (56 H III)				
	320	3 (25 Ed I)				
Hitchin	680	4 (53 H III)				
Hemel Hempstead			240	4 (30 Ed I)		
			60	6 (30 Ed I)		

TABLE I

	1st Gen.		2nd Gen.		3rd Gen.	
Broxbourne	120	4 (? Ed I)				
Marlin Farm	100	3 (3 Ed I)	120	3 (35 Ed I)		
(Northchurch)	120	3 (3 Ed I)				
Stevenage	1009	3 (3 Ed I)				
Betlow	120	4 (13 Ed I)				
Ware	536	4 (12 Ed I)				
Patmore Hall	160	4 (14 Ed I)				
Furneux Pelham	$66\frac{1}{2}$	4 (21 Ed I)				
	87	4 (21 Ed I)				
	$4\frac{1}{2}$	4 (21 Ed I)				
	4	4 (21 Ed I)				
Thorley	100	6 (22 Ed I)				
Chelsing	180	4 (24 Ed I)				
Gt. & Little Munden	140	4 (30 Ed I)	300	2 (27 Ed I)		
			180	4 (6 Ed II)		
Stocks			120	3 (27 Ed I)		
Weston			$663\frac{1}{2}$	4 (35 Ed I)		
			4	4 (12 Ed II)		
Weston by Baldock			140	4 (2 Ed II)		
Minsden			160	3 (32 Ed I)		
Almshoe			120	4 (32 Ed I)		
Lilley			120	3 (9 Ed II)	170	3 (7 Ed III)
Bengeo			200	3 (32 Ed I)		
Walterend Farm			120	3 (32 Ed I)		
(Theybridge)						
Thele (Stanstead			83	3 (12 Ed II)		
St. Margarets)						
Walhamstede			280	4 (15 Ed II)		
(Hitchin) &						
Redbourn						
Hoddesdon			180	2 (16 Ed II)		
Bennington			430	4 (17 Ed II)	300 (200)	4 (16 Ed III)
			204	2 (17 Ed II)		
Holwell			300	3 (17 Ed II)		
Holwell (Little)			68	3 (18 Ed II)	25	3 (1 Ed III)
Twendesbury			180	3 (18 Ed II)		
Essendon			200	3 (18 Ed ?)		
Bayford			160	$1\frac{1}{3}$ (18 Ed ?)	40	2 (1 Ed III)
					115	4 (19 Ed III) (or 2)
Cottered			60 (30)	2 (20 Ed II)	74	4 (19 Ed III)
Westwick Hall					305	2 (3 Ed III)
by St. Albans						
Studham					150	2 (2 Ed III)
(Chertewode: Beds)					30	4 (2 Ed III)
Barwythe					30	2 (2 Ed III)
(Studham: Beds)						
Cheshunt					160	3 (9 Ed III)
Knebworth					300	4 (9 Ed III)
Nuthampstead					321	4 (10 Ed III)

	1st Gen.		2nd Gen.		3rd Gen.	
Plessis					300(2/3)	4 (12 Ed III)
Buckland					300(2/3)	4 (12 Ed III)
Mardleybury					300(2/3)	4 (12 Ed III)
Therfield					180	4 (14 Ed III)
Harpsfield Hall					120(2/3)	4 (16 Ed III)
Hatherfeld					90	4 (16 Ed III)
Welles					120	6 (15 Ed III)
(Wellbury Ho:					160	4 (15 Ed III)
Offley)					160	2 (15 Ed III)
HUNTINGDONSHIRE						
Great Gidding	80	4 (56 H III)	40	3 (16 Ed II)		
	120	6 (25 Ed I)				
Dillington	260	4 (56 H III)	100	3 (16 Ed II)		
	600	4 (25 Ed I)				
Perry (West)	100	4 (56 H III)	140	2 (16 Ed II)		
Hamerton	408	6 (2 Ed I)				
	90	8 (10 Ed I)	120	2 (18 Ed II)	80	3 (20 Ed III)
Southoe	60	6 (2 Ed I)	80+	6 (30 Ed I)		
			150	6 (35 Ed I)		
Southoe Luvetot			80	4 (8 Ed II)		
Southoe & Orton Waterville					150	5 (23 Ed III)
Southoe & Boughton			10	6 (30 Ed I)		
Boughton (Southoe)					110	4 (23 Ed III)
Orton Longueville	80	6 (6 Ed I)				
Botolph Bridge & Orton	80	6 (20 Ed I)				
Botolph Bridge	80	6 (6 Ed I)				
Brampton	86	4 (16 Ed I)	100	6 (6 Ed II)	86	4 (2 Ed III)
					170	4 (9 Ed III)
					109	6 (22 Ed III)
					86	4 (23 Ed III)
Everton (Beds)	140	2½ (22 Ed I)	275	3 (15 Ed II)	240	4 (5 Ed III)
Alconbury & Weston	240	4 (23 Ed I)	250	4 (19 Ed II)		
Fen Stanton & Hilton	200	6 (23 Ed I)	170	4 (19 Ed II)		
Ellington Thorpe			60	4 (26 Ed I)	160	2 (23 Ed III)
Glatton			340	6 (28 Ed I)	52	7 (19 Ed III)
Caldecote (?)			140	4 (32 Ed I)	90	3 (4 Ed III)
					40	16 (5 Ed III)
					60	4 (24 Ed III)
Hemingford (Grey)			30	6 (1 Ed II)		
Yelling			200	4 (1 Ed II)	240	3 (16 Ed III)
Yelling, Hemingford, Turberville			120	3 (17 Ed II)		
Little Paxton			34	4 (3 Ed II)	75	4 (11 Ed III)
			40	2 (16 Ed II)	40	4 (18 Ed III)
					16	6 (19 Ed III)

	1st Gen.		2nd Gen.		3rd Gen.	
Great Paxton					80	4 (18 Ed III)
Offord Darcy			380	4 (15 Ed II)	388	2½ (5 Ed III)
Colne	60	6 (29 H III)				
Grafham			200	2 (16 Ed II)		
Conington	225	6 (53 H III)				
Kimbolton	800	4 (3 Ed I)				
	700	8½ (12 Ed I)				
Great Stukeley					240	4 (6 Ed III)
Lymage					200	4 (23 Ed III)
St. Neots					17	5 (23 Ed III)
Upwood					40	2 (23 Ed III)
Eynesbury					40	5 (23 Ed III)
Catworth	160	1½ (7 Ed I)				
Washingley	120	8 (16 Ed I)				
Diddington	162½	8 (18 Ed I)				
Gt. Staughton	572	6 (24 Ed I)				
	572?	4? (24 Ed I)				
Upton			72	4 (26 Ed I)		
Denton			70	4 (26 Ed I)		
Toseland			160	4 (1 Ed II)		
Offord Cluny			20	3 (7 Ed II)		
Great Gransden			100	4 (8 Ed II)		
Pidley			80	4 (12 Ed II)		
Folksworth			120	3 (15 Ed II)		
Chesterton					160	4 (18 Ed III)
					60	3 (19 Ed III)
LEICESTERSHIRE						
Ashby de la Zouch	529	6 (54 H III)			120 (80)	6 (11 Ed III)
					120 (80)	6 (21 Ed III)
Evington	600	6 (56 H III)			400	6 (9 Ed III)
Branston	240	4 (12 Ed I)	222	3 (29 Ed I)		
Groby	284	6 (16 Ed I)	80	4 (18 Ed II)	300(⅔)	2 (17 Ed III)
Kirby Ballards	39	4 (17 Ed I)	30	4 (31 Ed I)		
			75	4 (7 Ed II)		
			8	2 (15 Ed II)		
Hinckley	90	6 (25? Ed I)			128	4 (1 Ed III)
Earl Shilton	240	6 (25 Ed I)			240	3 (1 Ed III)
	74	6 (25 Ed I)				
Desford	222	5 (25 Ed I)			200	2 (1 Ed III)
Foston			137	17 (27 Ed I)		
			80?	6 (8 Ed II)		
Bottesford			192	12 (29 Ed I)	208 (160)	6 (17 Ed III)
Claybrook, Gt. & Little			54	6 (34 Ed I)	36	4 (9 Ed III)
Lowesby			140	3 (2 Ed II)	100	6 (12 Ed III)
Saddington			140	3½ (3 Ed II)	180 (120)	6 (11 Ed III)
			156	8 (9 Ed II)		
Burbage			120	4 (6 Ed II)	80	4 (9 Ed III)
Barwell			120	4 (6 Ed II)	80	4 (9 Ed III)
Wymeswold			72	3 (19 Ed II)	80	1 (3 Ed III)
Barkestone			90	8 (9 Ed II)		

	1st Gen.		2nd Gen.		3rd Gen.	
Whetstone	432	4 (39 H III)				
Cotestown	156	6 (39 H III)				
Barrow-upon-Soar	400	4 (1 Ed I)				
Beaumanor	100	8 (3 Ed I)				
Narborough	60	4 (12 Ed I)				
Normanton	112 (56)	12 (16 Ed I)				
Leicester	320	6 (25? Ed I)				
Witherley			128	6 (26 Ed I)		
Buckminster			456+	6 (26 Ed I)		
Houghton-on-the-Hill			120	2 (29 Ed I)		
Broughton			160	6 (29 Ed I)		
Willoughby Waterless			120	6 (29 Ed I)		
Saltby			80	3 (29 Ed I)	2 car (2/3)	60s (19 Ed III)
Redmile					86 (60)	4 (17 Ed III)
Knaptoft			160	4 (29 Ed I)		
Medbourne			85	5 (30 Ed I)		
Blaston			88	6 (30 Ed I)		
Drayton			10	6 (30 Ed I)		
Bringhurst			44	6 (30 Ed I)		
			2	4 (16 Ed II)		
Kirkby (Mallory)			60	4 (30 Ed I)		
Ab Kettleby			80	4 (31 Ed I)		
Twyford			37	4 (31 Ed I)		
Somerby			144	4 (31 Ed I)		
Pickwell			20	16 (31 Ed I)		
Lobthorpe (Lincs)			100	4 (32 Ed I)		
Gt. Easton			96	4 (32 Ed I)		
Croxton			72	9 (32 Ed I)		
South Croxton			300	4 (32 Ed I)		
Quenby			100	4 (32 Ed I)		
Baggrave			8	4 (32 Ed I)		
Burton Overy			165	4 (35 Ed I)		
Upton			216	6 (35 Ed I)		
Scheyle (Seal: Derbyshire)			240	4 (2 Ed II)		
Cotesbach			30	4 (3 Ed II)		
Newbold Saucey			57	3 (10 Ed II)		
			100	6 (3 Ed II)		
Lutterworth			103	4 (10 Ed II)		
Ashby Folville			80	4 (3 Ed II)		
Marefield South			153	5 (4 Ed II)		
Thornton			100	4 (4 Ed II)		
Donington			400	12 (4 Ed II)		
Nailstone			128	6 (6 Ed II)		
Muston			112	3 (9 Ed II)		
Aythelaxton (Aylestone?)			320	4 (10 Ed II)		
Saxby			116	4 (11 Ed II)		
Mowsley			160	4 (11 Ed II)		
			32	2 (19 Ed II)		
			100	2 (19 Ed II)		

	1st Gen.		2nd Gen.		3rd Gen.	
Gumley			100	3 (11 Ed II)		
			80	2 (19 Ed II)		
Kegworth			106	4 (15 Ed II)		
Church Langton			3	3 (15 Ed II)		
Neville Holt			20	4 (16 Ed II)		
			41	6 (30 Ed I)		
Seagrave			214	4 (19 Ed II)		
Gale Orton			140	2 (19 Ed II)		
Diseworth			214	4 (19 Ed II)		
Gt. Dalby			216	2 (19 Ed II)		
Congeston (Congerstone in Shakerstone?)					60	4 (1 Ed III)
Thrussington					192	4 (1 Ed III)
Melton Mowbray					100	4 (1 Ed III)
Freeby					80	4 (1 Ed III)
Prestwold					50 (0)	4 (3 Ed III)
Burton					10 (0)	4 (3 Ed III)
Hallaton					100	4 (4 Ed III)
Burton on the Wolds					82	2 (3 Ed III)
Cotes de Val					80	6 (4 Ed III)
Ashby (Town)					18	4 (4 Ed III)
Bitteswell					20	4 (4 Ed III)
Bosworth					89	4 (4 Ed III)
Castle Donington					360	4 (4 Ed III)
Odstone (in Shakerstone)					200 (2/3)	4 (5 Ed III)
Newton Harcourt					160 1/2 (109 1/2)	4 (6 Ed III)
Keythorpe					60	4 (11 Ed III)
Hemington			160	3 (19 Ed II?)	30	3 (24 Ed III)
Overton (Quartermars)					2 car.	30s (?)
NORTHAMPTONSHIRE						
Newbottle	63	12 (39 H III)	100	6 (15 Ed II)	100	6 (5 Ed III)
	130	12 (39 H III)	80	3 (18 Ed II)		
	204	4 (56 H III)				
	200	4 (16 Ed I)				
Blatherwycke	30	4 (45 H III)	60	4 (34 Ed I)		
	300	6 (25 Ed I)	120	4 (34 Ed I)		
			120	4 (5 Ed II)		
			200	4 (16 Ed II)		
Doddington (Gt.)	35 1/2	8 (47 H III)	15	3 (5 Ed II)		
			50	4 (5 Ed II)		
			15	3 (34 Ed I)		
			50	3 (34 Ed II)		
Wadenhoe	310	6 (48 H III)			300 (2/3)	6 (9 Ed III)

	1st Gen.		2nd Gen.		3rd Gen.	
Faxton	277	6 (50 H III)	200	4 (10 Ed II)		
			100	4 (8 Ed II)		
			120	2 (14 Ed II)		
Easton	26	18 (52 H III)	384	4 (26 Ed I)	240 (100)	4 (4 Ed III)
(on the Hill?)					(140)	3 (4 Ed III)
					240	$2\frac{1}{2}$ (24 Ed III)
Naseby	480	6 (24 Ed I)	321	4 (35 Ed I)		
Harringworth	374	6 (11? Ed I)	374	6 (27? Ed I)		
Wicken	63	10 (4 Ed I)			240	6 (19 Ed III)
Torpel	100	12 (5 Ed I)			239	6 (4 Ed III)
Upton	110	6 (5 Ed I)	120	6 (8 Ed II)	240	4 (4 Ed III)
	160	7 (8 Ed I)			200 ($\frac{2}{3}$)	6 (21 Ed III)
					240	2 (24 Ed III)
					36 (24)	4 (23 Ed III)
Cotterstock	180	12 (5 Ed I)	227	8 (30 Ed I)		
	$120\frac{1}{2}$	8 (18 Ed I)				
Weldon					300	6 (15 Ed III)
Walton					100	6 (5 Ed III)
					192 ($\frac{1}{2}$)	2 (19 Ed III)
Puxley	15 ( )	6 (6 Ed I)			$13\frac{1}{2}$ ( )	4 (14 Ed III)
	12	6 (6 Ed I)			10	3 (14 Ed III)
Islip	180	6 (6 Ed I)	17	8 (2 Ed II)		
Passenham	243	6 (6 Ed I)			300	4 (1 Ed III)
					21	80 (1 Ed III)
Plumpton	56	6 (7 Ed I)	86	4 (1 Ed II)		
Corby	220	4 (8 Ed I)	63	4 (10 Ed II)	180	3 (9 Ed III)
Barnwell	320 (30)	10 (9 Ed I)				
	(90)	6 (9 Ed I)	210	6 (15 Ed II)		
	(200)	4 (9 Ed I)				
Mears Ashby			36	5 (18 Ed II)	40	4 (21 Ed III)
					60	4 (21 Ed III)
Castle Ashby					160 (120)	4 (23 Ed III)
Dallington	180	6 (12 Ed I)			($133\frac{1}{2}$?)	6 (20 Ed III)
	$66\frac{1}{2}$	6 (12 Ed I)				
Slapton	154	5 (12 Ed I)			100 ($\frac{2}{3}$)	6 (20 Ed III)
	294	4+ (12 Ed I)				
Titchmarsh	410	6 (15 Ed I)	400	6 (8 Ed II)	480 ($\frac{2}{3}$)	6 (21 Ed III)
			480	10 (8 Ed II)		
Westpery	72	5 (16 Ed I)			400	3 (20 Ed III)
(Paulerspury)	5	6 (16 Ed I)			500	3 (23 Ed III)
Little Oakley	390	6 (18 Ed I)	240	4 (30 Ed I)	120	3 (23 Ed III)
			40	$3\frac{1}{2}$ (30 Ed I)		
			80	4 (16 Ed II)		
Great Oakley					60	2 (23 Ed III)
East Carlton	160	4 (18 Ed I)	100	4 (30 Ed I)	50	2 (23 Ed III)
			10+3	3 (16 Ed II)		
Great Houghton					120	4 (13 Ed III)
					40 ($\frac{2}{3}$)	6 (20 Ed III)
					200	2 (23 Ed III)
					46	4 (23 Ed III)
					($34\frac{1}{2}$)	
					50	3 (24 Ed III)
					($33\frac{1}{2}$)	

TABLE I

		1st Gen.		2nd Gen.		3rd Gen.
Little Houghton	160	8 (18 Ed I)	170	6 (30 Ed I)		
Chipping Warden	510	6 (20 Ed I)			? ($^1/_2$)	6 (8 Ed III)
Braybrooke	160	6 (20 Ed I)			81	4 (18 Ed III)
					40 (26$^2/_3$)	4 (18 Ed III)
Halefield Lodge	44	6 (20 Ed I)	40	6 (33 Ed I)	40 (26$^1/_3$)	4 (18 Ed III)
			20	4 (11 Ed II)		
Finedon	50	6 (21 Ed I)	27	6 (30 Ed I)		
	32	6 (22 Ed I)	10	6 (30 Ed I)		
Sulgrave	96	6 (22 Ed I)	52	4 (34 Ed I)	168 (84)	12 (18 Ed III)
					40	3 (18 Ed III)
Thorpe (?)					120 ($^1/_2$)	4 (17 Ed III)
Pattishall			172	7 (32 Ed I)	200	4 (10 Ed III)
					200 ($^1/_2$)	4 (22 Ed III)
Culworth	60	4 (24 Ed I)			60 ($^1/_2$)	3 (5 Ed III)
					120 ($^1/_2$?)	6 (5 Ed III)
Weston	240	6 (25 Ed I)	164	4 (15 Ed II)	63	6 (15 Ed III)
Weston Pynkney					34	3 (4 Ed III)
(Pinkney Moreton)					32	6 (17 Ed III)
Higham Ferrers			400$^1/_2$	4 (26 Ed I)	378$^1/_2$	8 (1 Ed III)
Rushton			379?	6 (26 Ed I)	379$^1/_2$	6 (1 Ed III)
					(189$^1/_2$$^1/_3$)	
Raunds			291	6 (26 Ed I)	291	8 (1 Ed III)
					(145?)	
Abington			192	6 (26 Ed I)	110 (100)	4 (23 Ed III)
Crick			96	4 (26 Ed I)	120	6 (1 Ed III)
			104	3 (28 Ed I)		
Wakerley			180	4 (27 Ed I)	400 ($^2/_3$)	3 (21 Ed III)
Little Weldon			56	12 (28 Ed I)	78	4 (14 Ed III)
			70	5 (10 Ed II)		
Burton Latimer			50	4 (29 Ed I)	60	4 (1 Ed III)
			80	4 (7 Ed II)	53	3 (6 Ed III)
			80	4 (17 Ed II)		
Potterspury	340	6 (25 Ed I)	200	6 (29 Ed I)		
			123	6 (9 Ed II)		
			120	6 (9 Ed II)		
			80	1 (18 Ed II)		
Stoke Albany			240	4 (29 Ed I)	300 (200)	4 (17 Ed III)
Yardley Gobion			300	4 (32 Ed I)	400 ($^2/_3$)	6 (22 Ed III)
			140	4 (6 Ed II)		
			180 (120)	4 (18 Ed II)		
Evenley			312	4 (32 Ed I)		
			100	3 (9 Ed II)		
East Haddon			100	8 (33 Ed I)	140	6 (4 Ed III)
Duston			60	4 (33 Ed I)	11	6 (23 Ed III)
			10	3 (15 Ed II)	18	4 (23 Ed III)
			24	2 (15 Ed II)		
			36	6 (1 Ed II)		
			170	6 (5 Ed II)		
Braunston			36	4 (33 Ed I)		
			120	3 (33 Ed I)		
			36	6 (5 Ed II)		
			100	6 (5 Ed II)		
Milton			200	6 (33 Ed I)	(200?)	4 (18 Ed III)

	1st Gen.		2nd Gen.		3rd Gen.	
Grafton (Regis)			116	10 (33 Ed I)		
			140	10 (33 Ed I)	40	4 (14 Ed III)
			7	6 (33 Ed I)		
Loddington			140	6 (33 Ed I)		
			120	3 (16 Ed II)		
Watford	51	6 (23 Ed I)	48	6 (10 Ed II)	190 (⅔)	4 (17 Ed III)
	12	6 (23 Ed I)			100 (⅔)	4 (19 Ed III)
Rothwell	266	6 (47? H III)	388½	6 (35 Ed I)		
	111	5 (47? H III)	379	4 (8 Ed II)		
	14	4 (47? H III)				
	390	6 (24 Ed I)				
Weedon Lois			56 (32)	6 (1 Ed II)	200	6 (17 Ed III)
			(24)	4 (1 Ed II)		
Towcester			300	6 (7 Ed II)		
			137	8 (7 Ed II)		
			20	6 (18 Ed II)		
			218	? (18 Ed II)		
			70 (46½)	6 (18 Ed II)		
Ashley			30	2 (9 Ed II)	120	4 (5 Ed III)
				as fallow		
			72	6 (15 Ed II)		
Desborough			156	4 (9 Ed II)	108 (½)	4 (18 Ed III)
Croughton	80	6 (20 Ed I)				
Radstone	200	6 (22 Ed I)				
Whitfield	24	6 (22 Ed I)				
Bulwick	216	3 (1? Ed I)				
Ashton	260	9 (2 Ed I)				
Byfield	59	6 (2 Ed I)				
Billing	276	12 (2 Ed I)				
Gretton	300	5 (2 Ed I)			160 (?)	4 (21 Ed III)
Horton	(195)	9 (2 Ed I)	10½ ( )	9 (29 Ed I)		
	17½	9 (29 Ed I)				
Glapthorn	70	9 (5 Ed I)				
Pilton	120	12 (5 Ed I)				
	24	7 (5 Ed I)				
Lowick	19	6 (6 Ed I)				
Silverstone	30	3 (6 Ed I)				
	9½ ( )	6 (6 Ed I)				
	4	6 (6 Ed I)				
Benefield			13½	6 (26 Ed I)		
Rockingham	460	6 (8 Ed I)				
Weekley	180	8 (8 Ed I)				
Wike (nr. Hartwell?)	232	4 (9 Ed I)				
Dodford	161	8 (10 Ed I)				
Stoke Bruerne	259½	4 (11 Ed I)				
Alderton	115	5 (11 Ed I)				
East Farndon	156	4 (16 Ed I)				
Nassington & Yarwell	220	10 (18 Ed I)			30	4 (5 Ed III)
Yarwell					29	4 (7 Ed III)
Fotheringhay	411	9 (18 Ed I)				
Cotton (Gretton)	70	6 (18 Ed I)			40	2 (23 Ed III)
Drayton	114	8 (20 Ed I)				
Brugbrook	420	6 (22 Ed I)				
	6	2 (24 Ed I)				
Greatworth	200	4 (23 Ed I)				

TABLE I

	1st Gen.		2nd Gen.		3rd Gen.	
Halse (Brackley)	425	12 (24 Ed I)	160	6 (26 Ed I)		
			416	4 (7 Ed II)		
Southwick			70	8 (26 Ed I)		
Wilby			80	4 (28 Ed I)		
Astcote			120	4 (28 Ed I)		
Ecton			40	6 (29 Ed I)		
			28	10 (29 Ed I)		
Welford			288	6 (29 Ed I)		
Northampton			300	4 (29 Ed I)		
Whittlewood			10½ ( )	2 (32 Ed I)		
Moreton Pinkney			200	2 (14 Ed II)	40	3 (19 Ed III)
					5	2½ (12 Ed III)
Long Buckby			270	12 (4 Ed II)	140 (⅔)	6 (17 Ed III)
Broughton			16	6 (7 Ed II)		
Astwell			80	3½ (8 Ed II)		
Brixsworth			295	6 (9 Ed II)		
Gayton			160	6 (9 Ed II)		
Creaton			60	6 (9 Ed II)		
			100	4 (10 Ed II)		
Haselbech			210	6 (9 Ed II)		
Falcutt			20	3 (9 Ed II)		
Moor End			20	4 (9 Ed II)		
			24	4 (9 Ed II)		
			20	4 (9 Ed II)		
			57	3 (9 Ed II)		
Lilford-cum-Wigsthorpe			200	6 (10 Ed II)		
Scaldwell			9½	4 (11 Ed II)		
Quinton			150	8 (11 Ed II)		
Harpole			103	4 (15 Ed II)	60 (½)	6 (8 Ed III)
					123 (⅔)	4 (12 Ed III)
					60 (⅔)	6 (20 Ed III)
Torpel (Ufford)					120	3 (24 Ed III)
Barton Seagrave			120	4 (15 Ed II)		
Earls Barton					60 (40)	4 (23 Ed III)
Seawell Farm (Blakesley)			18	3 (15 Ed II)		
Bucknell Wood (Abthorpe)			82 (53½)	5 (18 Ed II)		
Great Billing			120	4 (18 Ed II)	120	2 (23 Ed III)
Grendon			80 (54)	4 (18 Ed II)	5	4 (23 Ed III)
Wootton			141	4 (18 Ed II)	100	3½ (22 Ed III)
Denford			120 (80)	4 (19 Ed II)		
Chalcombe			250 (140) (110)	5 (19 Ed II)		
Brampton (Ash)			300	4 (19 Ed II)		
Pytchley	120	8 (25 Ed I)				
Moulton	400	6 (25 Ed I)			400	4 (8 Ed III)
					190 (⅔)	4 (17 Ed III)
Preston Wood					120	4 (1 Ed III)
					160 (½)	6 (9 Ed III)

	1st Gen.		2nd Gen.		3rd Gen.	
Stowe					340 (200)	8 (1 Ed III)
Kislingbury					400	6 (1 Ed III)
Chester Ho			50	6 (2 Ed II)	28	4 (1 Ed III)
Cosgrove					$12\frac{1}{2}$	3 (2 Ed III)
					18	12 (14 Ed III)
Cosgrove & Furtho					27+	4 (2 Ed III)
Cosgrove & Puxley					160	4 (2 Ed III)
					80	4 (2 Ed III)
Chelveston-cum-					$301\frac{1}{2}$ ($\frac{1}{2}$)	(2?) (4 Ed III)
Caldecott						
Kings Sutton					200	3 (5 Ed III)
Fawsley					96	6 (7 Ed III)
					22	$3\frac{1}{4}$ (7 Ed III)
Thorpe Mandeville					222 (111)	4 (8 Ed III)
Bozeat					160	4 (9 Ed III)
Deanshanger					200 ($\frac{2}{3}$)	6 (10 Ed III)
					33	3 (10 Ed III)
					10	12 (10 Ed III)
Kelmarsh					28	4 (11 Ed III)
					120 ($\frac{2}{3}$)	4 (11 Ed III)
Gt. Cransley					24	4 (11 Ed III)
Hardwick					120	3 (14 Ed III)
Bradden					90	3 (17 Ed III)
Alneston (Adstone)					12	6 (17 Ed III)
Irchester					140 ($\frac{2}{3}$)	6 (19 Ed III)
Oundle					60	10 (19 Ed III)
Wollaston					160 ($\frac{1}{2}$)	4 (20 Ed III)
Cogenhoe					?	3 (23 Ed III)
Great Harrowden					(60?) (40)	3 (23 Ed III)
Steane			130	3 (20 Ed II)		
Farthinghoe			88	3 (20 Ed II)		
Norton			120	3 (32 Ed I)	200	2 (17 Ed III)
			140	8 (1 Ed II)		
NOTTINGHAMSHIRE						
Wollaton	189	4 (1283)				
Cossall	50	4 (1283)				
Kingston (land in	28	6 (1294)	60	4 (1323)	60 (40)	3 (1336)
Ratcliffe on Soar)			10	4 (1223)		
Ratcliffe & Kingston	198	6 (1294)	10	4 (1322)		
Ratcliffe on Soar	192	$5\frac{1}{2}$ (1285-6)	300	4 (1308)		
	240	$5\frac{1}{2}$ (1285-6)				
	92	4 (1271-2)				
Ratcliffe on Trent					149	4 (1327)
Staythorpe	24	6 (1288)			300 ($\frac{2}{3}$)	5 (1341)
Markham Clinton	140	7 (1288-9)				
	120	6 (1301)				
Marnham	30	4 (1288-9)				
Scarthing Moor	24	4 (1288-9)				
Skegby (Marnham)			84	3 (1308)		
Scheggehagh (Marnham)	56	4 (1288-9)				

TABLE I

	1st Gen.		2nd Gen.		3rd Gen.	
Stoke (East)	100	5 (1289)				
Tuxford	276	7 (1291-2)				
	330½	8 (1291-2)				
	143½	4 (1297)				
	60	6 (1301)				
	60	3 (1301)				
Balderton	128 (86)	12 (1293)	128	6 (1305-6)		
Cuckney	60	4 (1294-5)				
Sutton	140	6 (1274-5)				
	120	4 (1271)				
Warsop	100	3 (1274-5)			80 (⅓)	2 (1328)
Worksop					200	6? (1332)
Eakring	180	4 (1294-5)				
Gringley	80 (pieces)	8 (1278)				
Orston	512	9 (1242)				
Carlton in Lindrick	58	12 (1244)				
Bothamsall	50	4 (1245-6)				
Nettleworth Manor	46	20 (1249)	30	4 (now Nil Waste 1321)		
			10	4 (now Nil Waste 1321)		
Kneesall	287	8 (1263)	240	6 (1311)		
Toton	144	6½ (1271-2)	60	6 (1308)		
Stapleford	110	6 (1297)	80	4 (1324)		
Car Colston	90	6 (1298)				
Langar	400 or 360	6 (1298)	300	6 (1314)	210 (166½)	6 (1328)
					60 (⅔)	1 (Past. 1328)
Gameston	180	3 (1298)				
Grove	80	1 (1299) (gross)				
Lambley	80	4 (1298-9)				
Cromwell	80	4 (1298-9)				
Gonalston	338	6 (1299)			18	6 (1329)
					180	6 (1343)
Widmerpool	252	4 (1299?)			240	4 (1329)
Strelley	120	6 (1301-2)				
Stoke Bardolph			80	3 (1304)	92	4 (1329)
Kirkby			116¾	4 (1310)		
Wiverton Hall			63	6 (1313)		
Epperstone			220	6 (1314)	125 (⅔)	6 (1328-9)
East Bridgeford			310	4 (1317)		
East & West Leake			200	4 (1323)		
Saxondale			72	4 (1323)		
Kingshaugh Ho.			200	4 (1324)	200	4 (1329)
Staunton-in-the-Vale			140	6 (1326)		
Eaton			110	3 (1326)		
Egmanton			200	6 (1326)		
Bunny			(100)(73)	4 (1326)		
Clifton					120	4 (1327)
Wilford					60	4 (1327)
Hucknall Torkard					30	3 (1329)
Weston					16	4 (1329)

	1st Gen.		2nd Gen.		3rd Gen.	
Grimston Hill					100	2 (1347)
(Wellow)					150	4 (1330)
Brinsley					63 (40)	6 (1331)
					60 (½)	2 (1345)
					63 (40)	6 (1321)
Grassthorpe					176 (⅔)	6 (1332)
Perlethorpe					200	2 (1333)
Caunton					200	6 (1334-5)
Barton in Fabis					200	12 (1334-5)
Arnold					80	6 (1335)
North Leverton					120 (⅔)	6 (1341)
Harworth					20 (+?)	3 (1340)
Mansfield					12 (8)	2 (1339)
Wansley					20 (⅔)	2 (1337)
					30	2 (1337)
Wiverton Hall,					65	3 (1337)
Barnstone & Tithby						(Entry Twice)
Trowell					30 (⅔)	? (1345)
Thorney					18	6 (1323-4)
Granby					100	4 (1326-27)
North Muskham			80	4 (1325)		
Laxton	240	10 (1287)				
	240	6 (1252)				
	54	6 (1252)				
	180	6 (1288-9)				
	175	6 (1297)				
RUTLAND						
Stretton	172	3 (44 H III)	192	3 (19 Ed II)		
			62	4 (15 Ed II)		
Little Casterton			90	6 (26 Ed I)	185	4 (10 Ed III)
					185	4 (18 Ed III)
Casterton			160	4 (29 Ed I)		
Oakham			270	20 (28 Ed I)	270	20 (21 Ed III)
Whissendene			140	4 (18 Ed II)	198	6 (10 Ed III)
					160	6 (23 Ed III)
					112	3 (23 Ed III)
Preston & Uppingham	324½	4 (24 Ed I)				
Barrowden			223	5 (26 Ed I)		
			208	6 (9 Ed II)		
Stoke Dry			112	6 (31 Ed I)		
Haliok (Holy Oak, Leics?)			38	6 (34 Ed I)		
Egleton					513	12 (21 Ed III)
Ashwell			120	6 (8 Ed II)		
Barrow			80	4 (9 Ed II)		
Greetham			80	6 (9 Ed II)		
Ketton			54	6 (16 Ed II)		

TABLE I

	1st Gen.		2nd Gen.		3rd Gen.	
Glaston			240	4 (20 Ed II)		
Exton					150 (100)	4 (4 Ed III)
Ryhall					85	6 (4 Ed III)
Essedine					150 (100)	4 (8 Ed III)
Upper Hambleton					320	6 (12 Ed III)
Market Overton					227	10 (12 Ed III)
Langham					388	12 (21 Ed III)
Seaton					40 ($^2/_3$)	2 (32 Ed III)

MEADOW

GENERAL REMARKS ON TABLE II

The fine network of streams observable on the relief maps of the East Midlands explains how meadow appeared almost as often as arable in the extents of the Inquisitions Post Mortem. At the same time, as largely a natural resource rather than the product of husbandry in the manner of arable cultivation, the occurrence of meadow in the extent does not simply follow that of arable. Some large and reasonably wealthy estates recorded little or no meadow in the Inquisitions. On the whole, the sizes of the meadow noted in the following table are so small relative to their estates that these meadows may be said to reflect quite local conditions in contrast with the common arable patterns following upon wide regions of clay, etc. Given the uneven incidence of meadow with respect both to geography and specific estates, the wide range of similar valuations for meadow can only be explained by market forces. In some instances of overall well endowed estates, meadow was valuable when arable was valuable. Also, some quite small units were exceptionally valuable — perhaps indicating a different, that is more actual rent evaluation. It would also appear that meadow frequently deteriorated in value by the third generation along with the general fall in value of arable.

While on the whole values of meadow did not seem to vary with amounts and values of arable, or with the size of the meadow itself, there are common ranges of meadow values that indicate a pattern of comparative county wealth not unlike the arable pattern. Northants appears with a good range of 12d, 24d and 36d values. Leicestershire by contrast has largely the 12d and 24d values only. Herts has a higher range of values than Leicestershire, though still well below Northants. Hunts is closer to Northants than is Herts. For Bucks it is difficult to generalize since large portions of the county are as valuable as Northants in meadow, though extensive regions were quite poor. For Beds it is also difficult to generalize since meadow value entries are so few in relation to the size of the county, but the tendency is towards lesser values than those obtaining for Northants.

TABLE II *SUMMARY*

	ENTRIES				ACREAGE			
	Generation				Generation			
County	1st	2nd	3rd	Total	1st	2nd	3rd	Total
Bedford	36	54	49	139	534	516	400¼	1450¼
Bucks	67	98	84	249	1498	1318¼	1197¾	4014
Herts	41	56	30	127	469½	638¼	287½	1395
Hunts	22	22	20	64	369	372¾	607¼	1349
Leics	15	53	32	100	274	769¼	548	1591¼
Northants	67	96	90	253	1540	1573¾	1422¼	4536
Notts	32	25	30	87	484½	497	386	1367½
Rutland	3	17	9	29	42	227½	397½	666
	Grand Total 1048				Grand Total 16369			

TABLE II — *MEADOW*

VALUE — FREQUENCY

BEDFORDSHIRE

1st Generation

Values:	3/4	5 1/2	8	12	16	18	20	22	24	30	36	42
Frequency:	1	1	1	4	2	7	2	1	8	2	6	1

2nd Generation

Values:	5	10	12	15	16	18	24	30	32	36	40	48
Frequency:	1	1	11	1	1	8	17	2	2	9	1	2

3rd Generation

Values:	4	6	8	10	12	15	16	18	24	30	32
Frequency:	1	4	1	1	20	1	1	9	8	2	1

BUCKINGHAMSHIRE

1st Generation

Values:	3	6	8	10	12	15	16	18	20	24	30	36	48
Frequency:	1	1	2	2	16	1	1	11	3	22	1	5	1

2nd Generation

Values:	8	10	12	16	17	18	19	20	24	28	30	32?	36	40
Frequency:	2	2	21	2	1	21	1	4	27	1	1	1	7	1

Values:	48	60
Frequency:	3	2

3rd Generation

Values:	1	3	6	8	10	12	13	15	16	18	20	24	28	30	36	48
Frequency:	1	2	1	2	1	20	1	1	2	21	1	23	1	1	4	1

TABLE II — *MEADOW*

VALUE — FREQUENCY

HERTFORDSHIRE

Ist Generation

Values:	6	8	12	16	18	20	30	36	48	65
Frequency:	1	1	6	2	5	2	2	1	1	1

2nd Generation

Values:	3	8	12	15	18	24	30	36	40
Frequency:	1	1	8	1	10	30	1	4	1

3rd Generation

Values:	6	8	9	12	16	18	20	24	30	36	42
Frequency:	2	1	1	2	1	7	1	11	2	1	1

HUNTINGDONSHIRE

Ist Generation

Values:	7	12	17	20	24	27	36	48
Frequency:	1	6	1	1	7	1	3	2

2nd Generation

Values:	12	18	20	24	38	60
Frequency:	5	3	1	12	1	1

3rd Generation

Values:	6	10	12	18	24
Frequency:	1	3	10	2	6

TABLE II — *MEADOW*

VALUE — FREQUENCY

LEICESTERSHIRE

1st Generation

Values:	8	12	16	18	24	30	36
Frequency:	1	1	4	1	6	1	1

2nd Generation

Values:	4	6	10	12	14	16	18	20	24	30	32	36	48
Frequency:	2	2	1	15	1	1	8	2	15	1	2	4	1

3rd Generation

Values:	5	6	12	16	18	24	29	30	48
Frequency:	1	3	14	1	6	4	1	1	1

NORTHAMPTONSHIRE

1st Generation

Values:	12	14	15	16	18	24	27	30	32	36	48
Frequency:	5	1	1	1	5	33	1	5	1	10	2

2nd Generation

Values:	3	4	6	8	10	12	15	16	18	20	24	30	32	36
Frequency:	1	1	2	2	1	18	2	1	10	2	38	5	2	6

Values:	48	60	80
Frequency:	2	2	1

3rd Generation

Values:	6	8	10	12	16	18	24	30	36	40	48	120
Frequency:	6	2	1	21	3	4	34	4	7	2	1	1

TABLE II — *MEADOW*

VALUE — FREQUENCY

NOTTINGHAMSHIRE

1st Generation

Values:	8	12	16	18	20	24	30	36	$37^1/_2$	48
Frequency:	1	3	1	6	3	8	1	7	1	1

2nd Generation

Values:	6	12	18	24	30	36
Frequency:	1	6	4	10	3	1

3rd Generation

Values:	6	8	10	12	15	18	24	30	40	48
Frequency:	2	3	3	5	1	5	8	1	1	1

RUTLAND

1st Generation

Values:	10	15	24
Frequency:	1	1	1

2nd Generation

Values:	8	15	18	24	30	36	42
Frequency:	2	1	4	2	3	4	1

3rd Generation

Values:	3	4	6	18	24	30	36	48
Frequency:	1	1	2	3	7	1	1	1

TABLE II. — *MEADOW*

	1st Gen.		2nd Gen.		3rd Gen.	
BEDFORDSHIRE						
Keysoe	20	24 (23 Ed I)	8	10 (9 Ed II)		
	20	24 (24 Ed I)	16	24 (17 Ed II)		
Cainhoe	15	16 (15 Ed I)	4	24 (4 Ed II)	10	12 (23 Ed III)
	48	18 (1273)	8	12 (12 Ed II)	7	8 (24 Ed III)
			4	12 (18 Ed II)		
			4	12 (19 Ed II)		
Moggerhanger	6	12 (17 Ed I)				
Kempston	15½	24 (18 Ed I)			15	12 (22 Ed III)
Chanston (Roxton)	13	36 (18 Ed I)	11	36 (30 Ed I)		
			2	24 (5 Ed II)		
Stanbridge	8	18 (20 Ed I)				
Eaton (Bray)	8	36 (22 Ed I)				
	54¾	30 (1274)	52	24 (27 Ed I)		
Sandy	21	42 (22 Ed I)				
Tempsford	1½	¾ (22 Ed I)				
Aspley Guise	12	24 (23 Ed I)				
Wootton	14	24 (23 Ed I)			3	12 (8 Ed III)
					2	12 (9 Ed III)
					2	12 (10 Ed III)
Flitwick	16	16 (24 Ed I)				
Woodhill	6	8 (24 Ed I)	½	24 (1 Ed II)	20	30 (10 Ed III)
					20	30 (22 Ed III)
Westoning	30	18 (25 Ed I)	21	12 (15 Ed II)		
Campton	52½	12 (25 Ed I)				
Houghton (Conquest)			6	18 (26 Ed I)		
Wymington			4	24 (26 Ed I)	?	18 (21 Ed III)
					1½	32 (25 Ed III)
					1½	12 (23 Ed III)
Luton			4	24 (27 Ed I)	2½	12 (2 Ed III)
			2	40 (34 Ed I)	4	18 (4 Ed III)
					3	6 (23 Ed III)
Luton			3	24 (32 Ed I)	6	24 (5 Ed III)
			1	12 (33 Ed I)		
Wood Croft (Luton)	6	12 (16 Ed I)			3	12 (20 Ed III)
Streatley			2	12 (29 Ed I)		
Higham Gobion			24	12 (29 Ed I)		
Dilwick			15	15 (30 Ed I)		
Cardington			5	24 (11 Ed II)		
Renhale	5	36 (1286)	6	5 (30 Ed I)		
Warden	5	22 (1280)				
(Gravenhurst)	4½	24 (1281)	1½	32 (32 Ed I)	2	12 (9 Ed III)
	4½	5½ (9 Ed I)	½	32 (32 Ed I)	1	18 (17 Ed III)
Dunton (by					4	18 (7 Ed III)
Biggleswade						
Ravensden			10	36 (32 Ed I)		
Odell			10	48 (32 Ed I)		
Odell (Little)			13½	48 (32 Ed I)		
			2	24 (32 Ed I)		
Wootton Pillinge			2½	30 (2 Ed II)		

TABLE II

	1st Gen.		2nd Gen.		3rd Gen.	
Cople			1+	36 (2 Ed II)		
Thurleigh			9	18 (1 Ed II)		
Brogborough			4	18 (1 Ed II)		
Wreste Park			6	18 (1 Ed II)		
Stagsden	16	18 (1283)	5	24 (4 Ed II)	8	12 (8 Ed III)
					1 1/2	18 (20 Ed III)
Millbrook	26	36 (1285)	10	24 (4 Ed II)	16	18 (4 Ed III)
Cotes (Eastcott)	20	36 (1285)	9	24 (4 Ed II)	20	24 (7 Ed III)
Ampthill			5	24 (4 Ed II)	6	12 (23 Ed III)
Haynes			13	36 (5 Ed II)	15	24 (1 Ed III)
Stotfold			5	36 (5 Ed II)	7	18 (1 Ed III)
Willington			10	36 (5 Ed II)	15	24 (1 Ed III)
Bletsoe			8	18 (6 Ed II)		
Bromham	8	20 (1278)				
	4	20 (1286)				
Blunham			40	16 (6 Ed II)		
Wyboston			5	18 (10 Ed II)		
			5	24 (10 Ed II)		
			3	30 (17 Ed II)		
Yelden			24	36 (11 Ed II)		
Northill	9	18 (18 Ed I)	6	24 (11 Ed II)		
Wilden	7 1/2	24 (1269)	2	12 (11 Ed II)	4	6 (23 Ed III)
			4	18 (15 Ed II)		
Meppershall			10	12 (13 Ed II)	10	12 (5 Ed III)
Arlesey			2	12 (15 Ed II)	5	12 (5 Ed III)
Harrold			20	36 (17 Ed II)		
Santon Barn			15	36 (17 Ed II)		
Podington			12	24 (17 Ed II)		
Shillington					8	24 (6 Ed III)
Toddington					31	6 (7 Ed III)
Sudbury					6	12 (7 Ed III)
					6	12 (8 Ed III)
					8	12 (22 Ed III)
Eyworth	4 1/4	18 (1282)				
	3 1/2	12 (1284)			6	15 (8 Ed III)
Henlow					6	12 (8 Ed III)
Milton Ernest					4	12 (8 Ed III)
Langford					20	24 (10 Ed III)
					20	24 (22 Ed III)
Sundon					16	18 (12 Ed III)
Turvey					1/2	16 (14 Ed III)
					3	18 (20 Ed III)
Beeston					2	12 (16 Ed III)
Stevington	24 1/2	24 (1264)			14	24 (23 Ed III)
Sutton					6 1/2	6 (23 Ed III)
	7	18 (20 Ed I)			1	10 (24 Ed III)
					20	12 (9 Ed III)
Hockliffe					6 1/4	4 (24 Ed III)
Radwell	17	36 (1266)				
Wrestlingworth	1	30 (1271)				
Flitton			10 1/2	12 (17 Ed II)		

		1st Gen.		2nd Gen.		3rd Gen.
BUCKINGHAMSHIRE						
Padbury	20	24 (32 H III)				
	16	24 (22 Ed I)				
Chalfont St. Giles					6	12 (23 Ed III)
Moulsoe	4	20 (36 H III)				
Fulmer	3	8 (38 H III)				
Datchet	34	16 (38 H III)				
	16	24 (38 H III)			41	12 (6 Ed III)
	8	12 (24 Ed I)				
Medenham	48	24 (48 H III)	30	24 (19 Ed II)	20	36 (21 Ed III)
	16	18 (15 Ed I)				
Chesham Bois	3	18 (24 Ed I)	4	24 (4? Ed I)	5	15 (13 Ed III)
Whitchurch	30	12 (48 H III)			8	12 (5 Ed III)
	20	12 (24 Ed I)				
Little Linford			16	36 (30 Ed I)	20	18 (12 Ed III)
Linford	12	24 (51 H III)				
Great Linford					18	13 (12 Ed III)
Edlesborough	13½	24 (24 Ed I)	3	12 (5 Ed II)	20	8 (8 Ed III)
					6	18 (9 Ed III)
					4½	18 (21 Ed III)
Risborough	20	48 (56 H III)	30	48 (28 Ed I)		
Burnham & Eton	27	8 (56 H III)				
Burnham					10	24 (1 Ed III)
					8	24 (1 Ed III)
Hitcham	30	12 (20 Ed I)				
Hitcham & Losmere					3	24 (12 Ed III)
Losmere	11	12 (20 Ed I)				
Newport Pagnell	71	24 (1 Ed I)			20	18 (12 Ed III)
	50	24 (19 Ed I)				
Hillesdon	20	36 (2 Ed I)				
	10	24 (20 Ed I)				
Wavendon	11	36 (? Ed I)			8	18 (7 Ed III)
Haversham	37½	36 (2 Ed I)	12	24 (34 Ed I)	31	12 (9 Ed III)
			36	24 (19 Ed II)	20	24 (21 Ed III)
Tyringham	50	20 (2 Ed I)				
Pirney (Astwood)	3	10 (2 Ed I)				
Quainton	18	12 (3 Ed I)				
	10	24 (23 Ed I)				
Linslade & Southcott	9	24 (14 Ed I)				
Leckhampstead	1	24 (7 Ed I)	1¾	12 (10 Ed II)		
Great Leckhampstead	6	30 (8 Ed I)	12	12 (32 Ed I)		
Thornton	16	24 (7 Ed I)				
Wycombe	7	24 (9 Ed I)			2	24 (5 Ed III)
Buckland	12	12 (12 Ed I)			7	24 (8 Ed III)
					5	18 (8 Ed III)
Fulbrook	6	24 (12 Ed I)	4	18 (33 Ed I)	8	24 (8 Ed III)
	6	18 (13 Ed I)				
Cublington	15	24 (12 Ed I)	20	20 (33 Ed I)	8	24 (20 Ed III)
Shabbington			6	24 (6 Ed II)		
Chelmscott	30	18 (13 Ed I)			20	30 (20 Ed III)
Grove	12	20 (13 Ed I)				

	1st Gen.		2nd Gen.		3rd Gen.	
Hambleden			20	40 (12 Ed II)	20	24 (12 Ed III)
					2	10 (12 Ed III)
					12	1 (12 Ed III)
					1	18 (12 Ed III)
Grendon	16	24 (25 Ed I)	20	18 (29 Ed I)	32	18 (7 Ed III)
Underwood			$19\frac{1}{4}$	17 (32 Ed I)		
			10	24 (4 Ed II)		
			$22\frac{1}{2}$	10 (18 Ed II)		
Crafton	6	12 (14 Ed I)	5	12 (32 Ed I)		
	5	12 (20 Ed I)				
Ellesborough	6	12 (16 Ed I)				
Chesham	4	12 (15 Ed I)	3	10 (30 Ed I)	10	3 (5 Ed III)
					18	3 (5 Ed III)
Gt. Missenden	$7\frac{1}{2}$	18 (18 Ed I)			$3\frac{3}{4}$	12 (6 Ed III)
					6	18 (11 Ed III)
Missenden	8	18 (20 Ed I)	4	12 (29 Ed I)		
Little Missenden	2	24 (33 H III)				
Waddesdon	4	36 (20 Ed I)				
Seabrook	8	12 (21 Ed I)				
Drayton Beauchamp			2	24 (6 Ed II)		
Drayton Parslow	6	12 (21 Ed I)				
Hartwell	8	18 (22 Ed I)				
	11	18 (23 Ed I)				
Aylesbury	6	12 (23 Ed I)			200	24 (12 Ed III)
	134	18 (25 Ed I)				
	[137	6 (25 Ed I)]				
Hardwick	5	12 (25 Ed I)	8	24 (3 Ed II)		
			16	32? (4 Ed II)		
			$10\frac{1}{2}$	20 (9 Ed II)		
Weedon			5	12 (30 Ed II)	8	12 (23 Ed III)
Sherington	8	36 (24 Ed I)	$\frac{3}{4}$	16 (29 Ed I)		
Chearsley	23	18 (24 Ed I)	26	18 (18 Ed II)		
Brickhill			6	18 (1 Ed II)		
Little Brickhill	14	24 (24 Ed I)	18	24 (9 Ed II?)		
			12	18 (35 Ed I)		
Wendover	34	3 (24 Ed I)	20	12 (30 Ed I)		
Wendover & Weston Turville					6	18 (5 Ed III)
Little Broughton	30	15 (25 Ed I)			6	18 (5 Ed III)
					25	18 (23 Ed III)
Broughton					4	12 (23 Ed III)
Kingsey			18	12 (26 Ed I)		
Hanslope			54	24 (26 Ed I)		
			$107\frac{1}{2}$	36 (9 Ed II)		
			60	36 (11 Ed II)		
			40	36 (18 Ed II)		
Dunton			6	12 (26 Ed I)		
			5	12 (16 Ed II)		
Feldham			10	18 (27 Ed I)		
Woodham			2	18 (27 Ed I)		
Amersham			12	24 (27 Ed I)	1	(8) (8 Ed III)
			2	12 (30 Ed I)	20	48 (10 Ed III)

		1st Gen.		2nd Gen.		3rd Gen.
Cippenham	40	10 (56 H III)	40	18 (28 Ed I)		
Iver			24	16 (32 Ed I)	29	12 (23 Ed III)
			16	18 (3 Ed II)		
Stoke Poges					2	28 (5 Ed III)
					12	36 (5 Ed III)
Woburn			10	12 (29 Ed I)		
Wingrave			8½	12 (29 Ed I)		
Marsworth			2	12 (30 Ed I)		
			2½	18 (35 Ed I)		
			2½	18 (4 Ed II)		
			13	24 (12 Ed II)		
Olney			6	24 (30 Ed I)	20	24 (17 Ed III)
Stoke Halling			6½	12 (32 Ed I)		
Adstock			5	30 (33 Ed I)	4	12 (10 Ed III)
Dorney			7	12 (33 Ed II)		
Stoke Goldington			8	24 (5 Ed II)	5	24 (1 Ed III)
			6	24 (33 Ed I)	1	12 (23 Ed III)
			7	36 (2 Ed II)		
Buckingham			30	24 (33 Ed I)		
			12	18 (20 Ed I)		
Ilmer			28	19 (34 Ed I)	8	24 (3 Ed III)
Stewkley			5	8 (35 Ed I)		
East Claydon	50	24 (25 Ed I)	8	12 (6 Ed II)		
Gt. Marlow			20	24 (35 Ed I)		
Marlow			32	24 (8 Ed II)		
Addington			6	12 (1 Ed II)	6	24 (3 Ed III)
La Waterhall			10	24 (1 Ed II)		
Eton			10	18 (1 Ed II)		
Stoke Hammond			4	12 (1 Ed II)		
			14	18 (17 Ed II)		
Snelson			16	18 (1 Ed II)		
Eythorpe			16	36 (2 Ed II)		
Weston Turville			6	36 (2 Ed II)	20	6 (23 Ed III)
			10	48 (9 Ed II)		
Gayhurst					6	12 (23 Ed III)
Farnham			2½	24 (3 Ed II)		
			2½	18 (10 Ed II)		
Lathbury	12	24 (15 Ed I)	8	24 (4 Ed II)		
			10	18 (10 Ed II)		
Holmer Green			4	12 (4 Ed II)	5	24 (9 Ed III)
Emberton			1	48 (5 Ed II)	4	36 (5 Ed III)
Ickford			10	24 (6 Ed II)		
Saunderton			¾	24 (6 Ed II)		
Dinton			15	24 (7 Ed II)		
Worminghall			4	8 (8 Ed II)		
Lavendon			10½	60 (9 Ed II)		
Chilton			15	60 (9 Ed II)		
Whelpley Hill			2	28 (15 Ed II)		
(Chesham)			4	12 (15 Ed II)		
La Burrow & Parmoor (Hambleden)			2	24 (17 Ed II)		
Workington (Waddesdon?)			2	20 (17 Ed II)		

TABLE II

	1st Gen.		2nd Gen.		3rd Gen.	
Simpson			31	24 (17 Ed II)		
Beachendon			12	18 (18 Ed II)	12	18 (1 Ed III)
Stantonbury			24	18 (18 Ed II)		
Stanton			14	18 (19 Ed II)		
Hardmead			8	24 (19 Ed II)		
Penn			1/2	20 (19 Ed II)		
Whaddon	42	12 (25 Ed I)			78	18 (7 Ed III)
Aston Sanford					4	18 (2 Ed III)
Aston Bernard (Mullins)					16	24 (3 Ed III)
Calverton					12	36 (5 Ed III)
Gt. & Little Kimble					4	18 (5 Ed III)
Gt. Kimble					6	12 (23 Ed III)
Hoggeston					7	12 (5 Ed III)
Gt. & Little Horwood					20	12 (23 Ed III)
Woolstone (Gt. & Little)					14	12 (23 Ed III)
Foscott					7	24 (7 Ed III)
Bradenham					6	18 (7 Ed III)
Singleborough	6	18 (25 Ed I)			3	24 (7 Ed III)
					3	24 (8 Ed III)
					3 1/2	20 (8 Ed III)
Easington			18	18 (35 Ed I)	10	18 (8 Ed III)
Westbury & Radclive					14	24 (9 Ed III)
Chenies (Isenhampstead)					21	18 (9 Ed III)
Preston					16	16 (13 Ed III)
					5	24 (17 Ed III)
Cowley					14	16 (12 Ed III)
Caldecote & Willen					4	12 (14 Ed III)
Chivery in Aston					6	12 (15 Ed IIII)
Wolverton	34	24 (32 H III)			20	24 (15 Ed III)
					20	18 (23 Ed III)
Dorton (by Brehulle)					8	18 (17 Ed III)
Northall					6	12 (18 Ed III)
Salden					8	12 (23 Ed III)
					6	24 (5 Ed III)
Milton Keynes					44	12 (23 Ed III)
HERTFORDSHIRE						
Hunsdon	20	24 (33 H III)				
	16	12 (25 Ed I)				
	10	18 (56 H III)				
	3	8 (56 H III)				
Sacombe	10	16 (37 H III)	9	36 (8 Ed II)	4	42 (7 Ed III)
	10	18 (11 Ed I)	8	24 (14 Ed II)		
	3 1/4	24 (17 Ed I)				

	1st Gen.		2nd Gen.		3rd Gen.	
Standon	15	24 (46? H III)	7½	24 (1 Ed II)	4	30 (15 Ed III)
	26½	24 (24 Ed I)	8	30 (8 Ed II)		
			28	36 (8 Ed II)		
			29	36 (35 Ed I)		
Meesden	16	18 (47 H III)	6	24 (7 Ed II)		
Albury	12	12 (47 H III)	14	12 (34 Ed I)		
	12	20 (55 H III)				
Flamstead	5	65 (48 H III)	4	24 (3 Ed II)	4	6 (11 Ed III)
			4	12 (9 Ed II)		
Hitchin	40¼	24 (53 H III)				
Hemel Hempstead			13	8 (30 Ed I)		
Sawbridgeworth	14	24 (56 H III)	4	24 (4 Ed II)		
	2	24 (56 H III)				
	16	24 (23 Ed I)	16	18 (15 Ed II)		
Pishobury	20	24 (22 Ed I)				
Broxbourne	3½	20 (? Ed I)				
Marlin Farm (Northchurch)	2	12 (3 Ed I)				
Little Berkhamsted	15	24 (23 Ed I)	22	24 (3 Ed II)	20	24 (11 Ed III)
			20	24 (9 Ed II)	2	18 (19 Ed III)
Berkhamsted	16	12 (56 H III)	14½	24 (32? Ed I)	24	(8) (? Ed III)
Walkern	17½	36 (8 Ed I)	8½	24 (6 Ed II)		
Gt. Wymondley	2	24 (11? Ed I)				
Wyddial	8	30 (12 Ed I)			4	24 (15 Ed III)
Great Gaddesden			6	18 (7 Ed II)		
Gaddesden			42¼	18 (15 Ed II)		
Wigginton	9	16 (12 Ed I)	20	12 (33 Ed I)	10	18 (20 Ed III)
Betlow	6	18 (13 Ed I)				
Ware	56	30 (12 Ed I)				
King's Walden					8	24 (3 Ed III)
Little Hormead			3	24 (7 Ed II)		
Hormead	16	24 (24 Ed I)	2	24 (7 Ed II)		
	3	12 (14 Ed I)	5	12 (4 Ed II)		
Rableyheath			3	18 (4 Ed II)	3?	24 (9 Ed III)
Watton at Stone	4½	24 (14 Ed I)			12	18 (3 Ed III)
Stapleford	7½	24 (14 Ed I)				
Patmore Hall	1½	12 (14 Ed I)				
Furneux Pelham	4	6 (21 Ed I)				
Thundridge	10	24 (21 Ed I)				
	5	48 (22 Ed I)				
Thorley	8	24 (22 Ed I)				
Pirton	10	24 (23 Ed I)	12	18 (33 Ed I)	5	24 (21 Ed III)
			6	24 (18 Ed II)		
Theobald St. (Oldenham)	5	18 (24 Ed I)	2	24 (27 Ed I)		
Chelsing	8	18 (24 Ed I)				
Pope's Hall (Buckland)	2	24 (24 Ed I)	1	24 (8 Ed II)		
Eastwick (atte Flore)					30	24 (15 Ed III)
Eastwick			8	12 (29 Ed I)		
			33	24 (11 Ed II)		
			5	24 (11 Ed II)		

TABLE II

	1st Gen.		2nd Gen.		3rd Gen.	
Weston			33	12 (35 Ed I)		
Kings Langley			4	24 (32 Ed I)		
Bengeo			40	24 (32 Ed I)		
Walterend Farm (Theybridge)			4	24 (32 Ed I)		
Bishops Hatfield			6	24 (32 Ed I)		
			6	24 (1 Ed II)		
Great Bishey Wood (Wheathampstead)			3	24 (34 Ed I)		
Bishey (Wood)					40	20 (4 Ed III)
					14	16 (4 Ed III)
Hertingfordbury			30	24 (3 Ed II)		
			10	24 (18 Ed II)		
Great Anstey			3	24 (7 Ed II)		
Little Anstey			2	24 (7 Ed II)		
Reed					1	24 (15 Ed III)
Stagenhoe			2	24 (9 Ed II?)		
Berwick			4	40 (12 Ed II)		
Thele (Stanstead St. Margarets)			2	18 (12 Ed II)		
Reden			5	15 (12 Ed II)		
Stanstead (Abbots)			3½	3 (12 Ed II)		
Walhamstede (Hitchin) & Redbourn			4	12 (15 Ed II)		
Hoddesdon			53	24 (16 Ed II)		
Bennington			14	36 (17 Ed II)	10	24 (16 Ed III)
			6	18 (17 Ed II)		
Holwell			14	24 (17 Ed II)		
			3	24 (17 Ed II)		
Little Holwell			3	12 (17 Ed II)	4	18 (1 Ed III)
Twendesbury			4	18 (18 Ed II)		
Essendon			8	18 (18 Ed II)		
Bayford			8	18 (18 Ed II?)	2	18 (19 Ed III)
Westwick Hall by St. Albans					4	9 (3 Ed III)
Studham					4	12 (2 Ed III)
(Chertewode) (Beds)					4	6 (2 Ed III)
Aston					6	12 (4 Ed III)
Cheshunt					20	24 (9 Ed III)
Knebworth					10	24 (9 Ed III)
Nuthampstead					14½	36 (10 Ed III)
Plessis					8	18 (12 Ed III)
Buckland					12	30 (12 Ed III)
Therfield					3	24 (14 Ed III)
Welles (Wellbury Ho: Offley)					1	18 (15 Ed III)
HUNTINGDONSHIRE						
Great Gidding	1	24 (25 Ed I)				
Dillington	12	24 (56 H III)	5	12 (16 Ed II)		
	20	12 (25 Ed I)				

	1st Gen.		2nd Gen.		3rd Gen.	
Hamerton	3	24 (2 Ed I)	$1\frac{1}{4}$	60 (18 Ed II)		
Southoe	3	48 (2 Ed I)	4	24 (30 Ed I)		
			$2\frac{1}{2}$	38 (35 Ed I)		
Southoe Luvetot			2	24 (8 Ed II)		
Southoe & Orton Waterville					2	10 (23 Ed III)
Southoe & Boughton			2	24 (30 Ed I)		
Boughton (Southoe)					4	12 (23 Ed III)
Orton Longueville	7	7 (6 Ed I)				
Botolph Bridge & Orton	16	36 (20 Ed I)				
Botolph Bridge	7	7 (6 Ed I)				
Brampton	15	24 (16 Ed I)	200	24 (6 Ed II)	15	12 (2 Ed III)
					205	24 (9 Ed III)
					$278\frac{1}{2}$	(22 Ed III)
					(163) ($\frac{1}{2}$)	24
					(115)	12
					15	12 (23 Ed III)
Weston	5	12 (33 H III)				
Sawtry	10	36 (47 H III)				
Everton (Beds)	2	12 (22 Ed I)	20	12 (15 Ed II)	20	12 (5 Ed III)
Alconbury & Weston	28	12 (23 Ed I)	20	24 (19 Ed II)	30	12 (23 Ed III)
Fen Stanton & Hilton	52	24 (23 Ed I)	20	24 (19 Ed II)		
Ellington Thorpe			$6\frac{1}{2}$	18 (26 Ed I)	4	12 (23 Ed III)
Glatton					1	12 (19 Ed III)
Caldecote			3	12 (32 Ed I)	4	18 (4 Ed III)
					1	18 (5 Ed III)
Hemingford (Grey)			12	24 (1 Ed II)		
Yelling & Hemingford, Turberville			10	18 (17 Ed II)		
Little Paxton			2	24 (3 Ed III)	$\frac{3}{4}$	12 (11 Ed III)
					$1\frac{1}{2}$	24 (18 Ed III)
Great Paxton					3	12 (18 Ed III)
Offord Darcy			10	24 (15 Ed II)	10	24 (5 Ed III)
Colne	4	12 (29 H III)				
Conington	$25\frac{1}{2}$	24 (53 H III)				
Kimbolton	60	24 (3 Ed I)				
	65	12 (12 Ed I)				
Great Stukeley					8	24 (6 Ed III)
Lymage					4	24 (23 Ed III)
St. Neots					1	10 (23 Ed III)
Upwood					3	6 (23 Ed III)
Catworth	3	27 (7 Ed I)				
Washingley	$7\frac{1}{2}$	36 (16 Ed I)				
Diddington	3	48 (18 Ed I)				
Great Staughton	30	20 (24 Ed I)	30	20 (26 Ed I)		
Denton			$1\frac{1}{2}$	12 (26 Ed I)		
Toseland			8	18 (17 Ed II)		
			4	24 (1 Ed II)		
Great Gransden			4	24 (8 Ed II)		

	1st Gen.		2nd Gen.		3rd Gen.	
Pidley			3	24 (12 Ed II)		
Folksworth			2	12 (15 Ed II)		
LEICESTERSHIRE						
Whetstone	20	16 (39 H III)				
Haleweton	2	36 (18 Ed I)				
Ashby de la Zouch	15	16 (59 H III)			12	18 (11 Ed III)
					12	18 (21 Ed III)
Evington	40	24 (56 H III)			100	29 (9 Ed III)
Barrow-upon-Soar	48	24 (1 Ed I)				
Beaumanor					10	24 (14 Ed III)
Thorpe Arnold	16	24 (5 Ed I)	38	12 (8 Ed II)		
	4	8 (5 Ed I)				
Branston	6	30 (12 Ed I)	22	24 (27 Ed I)		
Narborough	8	24 (12 Ed I)				
Groby	15	24 (16 Ed I)			11	12 (17 Ed III)
Normanton	15	12 (16 Ed I)	12	12 (9 Ed II)		
Kirby Ballards	5	18 (17 Ed I)	4	18 (31 Ed I)		
			2	14 (31 Ed I)		
			6	24 (7 Ed II)		
Leicester	44	24 (25? Ed I)				
Earl Shilton	16	16 (25? Ed I)			26	12 (1 Ed III)
Desford	20	16 (25? Ed I)			16	12 (1 Ed III)
Foston			10	36 (8 Ed II)		
Houghton-on-the-Hill			6	20 (29 Ed I)		
Willoughby Waterless			4 1/2	24 (29 Ed I)		
Bottesford			60	24 (29 Ed I)	60	12 (17 Ed III)
Redmile			10	24 (29 Ed I)	39	12 (17 Ed III)
Knaptoft			9	36 (29 Ed I)		
Drayton			2	18 (30 Ed I)		
Bringhurst			8	36 (30 Ed I)		
Kirkby (Mallory)			4 1/2	32 (30 Ed I)		
Ab Kettleby			5	24 (31 Ed I)		
Twyford			3	12 (31 Ed I)		
Pickwell			5	12 (31 Ed I)		
Holy Oaks			2	24 (31 Ed I)		
Lobthorpe (Lincs)			53	18 (32 Ed I)		
Gt. Easton			16	18 (32 Ed I)		
Croxton			3	18 (32 Ed I)		
Claxton (Long Clawson)			10	12 (33 Ed I)		
Burton Overy			20 1/4	24 (35 Ed I)		
Upton			9	20 (35 Ed I)		
Lowesby			5	24 (2 Ed II)	30	16 (12 Ed III)
Cotesbach			5	12 (3 Ed II)		
Lutterworth			10	12 (3 Ed II)		
			6 1/2	18 (10 Ed II)		
Ashby Folville			10	24 (3 Ed II)		
Saddington			10	12 (3 Ed II)	10	18 (11 Ed III)
			11 1/2	24 (9 Ed II)		
			3 1/2	30 (9 Ed II)		

	1st Gen.		2nd Gen.		3rd Gen.	
Thornton			10	48 (4 Ed II)		
Donington			85	24 (4 Ed II)		
Burbage			16	12 (6 Ed II)	8	18 (9 Ed III)
Barwell			16	12 (6 Ed II)	12	12 (9 Ed III)
Nailstone			20	12 (6 Ed II)		
Muston			12	12 (9 Ed II)		
Saxby			3	12 (11 Ed II)		
			2	12 (11 Ed II)		
Mowsley			2	16 (19 Ed II)		
			4	32 (19 Ed II)		
			6	36 (19 Ed II)		
Gumley			1	10 (11 Ed II)		
Kegworth			5	18 (15 Ed II)		
Long Whatton			5	12 (15 Ed II)		
Neville Holt			3/4	24 (16 Ed II)		
			3	24 (30 Ed I)		
Bringhurst			1 3/4	24 (16 Ed II)		
Seagrave			47	4 (19 Ed II)		
Gale Orton			40	6 (19 Ed II)		
Diseworth			21	18 (19 Ed II)		
Gt. Dalby			40	4 (19 Ed II)		
Congeston (Congerstone in Shakerstone?)					4	12 (1 Ed III)
Thrussington					15	24 (1 Ed III)
Melton Mowbray					12	24 (1 Ed III)
Freeby					8	18 (1 Ed III)
Prestwold					2	12 (3 Ed III)
Burton					6	12 (24 Ed III)
					4	6 (3 Ed III)
Wymeswold					4	6 (3 Ed III)
Burton on the Wolds					4	5 (3 Ed III)
					2	6 (3 Ed III)
Bosworth					4	12 (4 Ed III)
Castle Donington					70	30 (4 Ed III)
Odstone in Shakerstone					10	18 (5 Ed III)
Newton Harcourt					3	48 (6 Ed III)
Whitwick (in Coalville)					10	12 (14 Ed III)
					10	12 (23 Ed III)
Loughborough					20	24 (14 Ed III)
Hugglescote (Coalville)						12 (14 Ed III)
Arnesby					6	12 (14 Ed III)
Hose			40	6 (19 Ed II?)		
Barkestone			3	24 (8 Ed II)		
NOTTINGHAMSHIRE						
Wollaton	4 1/2	36 (1283)				
Cossall	7	36 (1283)				

TABLE II

	1st Gen.		2nd Gen.		3rd Gen.	
Ratcliffe on Soar	1	36 (1285-6)	10	24 (1308)		
	8 1/2	48 (1285-6)				
	10	24 (1294)	20	36 (1313)		
	3	37 1/2 (1271-2)				
Laxton	27	36 (1287)				
	7	24 (1287)				
	9	18 (1287)				
	34	36 (1252)				
	50	12 (1288-9)	26 1/2	18 (1297)	20	24 (1341)
Staythorpe	13	20 (1288)				
	10	16 (1288)				
Markham Clinton	20	18 (1288-9)	29	12 (1301)		
Marnham	8	12 (1288-9)				
Muskham					8	24 (1340)
Stoke East	18 1/2	24 (1289)				
Tuxford	16	30 (1291-2)				
	47 1/2	24 (1291-2)				
	18	20 (1291-2)				
	5	18 (1297)				
	5	12 (1301)				
	9 1/2	8 (1301)				
Balderton	10	24 (1293)	10	24 (1305-6)		
Cuckney	2	18 (1294-5)				
Headon	10	24 (1295)				
Sutton	30	24 (1274-5)				
	6	20 (1271)				
Warsop	2	18 (1274-5)			4	12 (1338)
Worksop					40	18 (1332)
Eakring	4	36 (1274-5)				
Orston	15 1/2	24 (1242)				
Bothamsall	15	18 (1245-6)				
Kneesall	23	36 (1263)	20	24 (1311)		
Hareston (Orston)			15	18 (1298)		
Langar			30	30 (1298)		
			30	30 (1314)		
Gameston			30	12 (1298)		
Grove			1	6 (1299)		
Lambley			3	12 (1298-9)		
Cromwell			40	24 (1298-9)		
Gonalston			62	24 (1299)	32	18 (1329)
					32	18 (1343)
Widmerpool			9	12 (1298)	6	6 (1329)
Strelley			3	18 (1301-2)		
Shelford			10	24 (1304)	8	12 (1329-30)
Stoke Bardolph			10	18 (1304)	7	24 (1329)
Skegby (Marnham)			30	24 (1308)		
Toton			20	30 (1308)		
Kirkby			15	12 (1310)		
Wiverton Hall			9	24 (1313)		
Epperstone			14	24 (1314)	9	24 (1328-9)
East Bridgeford			10 1/2	24 (1317)		
Hoveringham & Flinham			40	12 (1326)		
Kingshaugh Ho.					4	24 (1329)

	1st Gen.		2nd Gen.		3rd Gen.	
Hucknall Torkard					2	12 (1329)
Grimston Hall					2½	40 (1330)
Brinsley					15	8 (1331)
					12	8 (1345)
Grassthorpe					24	24 (1332)
Perlethorpe					20	12 (1333)
Caunton					15	30 (1334-5)
Barton in Fabis					20	48 (1334-5)
Arnold					20	24 (1335)
North Leverton					15	24 (1341)
Hartworth					10	15 (1340)
					2	10 (1337)
Wansley					6	10 (1337)
Wiverton Hall,					12	12 (1337)
Barnstone & Tithby					6	8 (1345)
Trowell					3	10 (1323-4)
Thorney					12	18 (1326-7)
Granby					6	6 (1326-7)
North Muskham					13½	18 (1325)
NORTHAMPTONSHIRE						
Newbottle	15	18 (39 H III)	4	12 (15 Ed II)	4	12 (5 Ed III)
	32	24 (56 H III)	6	30 (18 Ed II)		
	11	16 (16 Ed I)				
Blatherwycke	10	24 (25 Ed I)	2	12 (34 Ed I)		
			2	12 (5 Ed II)		
			6	18 (16 Ed II)		
Rothwell	34	36 (47? H III)	69	24 (35 Ed I)		
	21	24 (47? H III)	68½	24 (8 Ed II)		
	34½	18 (47? H III)				
	6½	15 (47? H III)				
Wadenhoe	17⅓	48 (48 H III)				
Faxton	10	18 (50 H III)	12	30 (10 Ed II)	18	30 (9 Ed III)
			6	24 (8 Ed II)		
			6	12 (14 Ed II)		
Easton (on-the-Hill)			24⅓	36 (26 Ed I)	40	36 (4 Ed III)
					16	18 (4 Ed III)
					40	6 (24 Ed III)
Croughton	2	24 (20 Ed I)				
Radstone	10	24 (22 Ed I)				
	15	12 (22 Ed)				
Naseby	23	24 (22 Ed I)	31	6 (35 Ed I)		
	33½	24 (24 Ed I)				
Bulwick	5	[24 (1 Ed I)]				
Harringworth	80½	[24 (1 Ed I)]	73½	24 [(27 Ed I)]		
Ashton	28	24 (2 Ed I)				
Byfield	3	18 (2 Ed I)				
Wicken	5	24 (4 Ed I)			10	24 (19 Ed III)
Torpel (Ufford)	50	24 (5 Ed I)			63	36 (4 Ed III)

	1st Gen.		2nd Gen.		3rd Gen.	
Upton	6	24 (5 Ed I)	8	6 (2 Ed II)	8	40 (4 Ed III)
	5	36 (8 Ed I)	6	24 (8 Ed II)	10	36 (21 Ed III)
					10	12 (24 Ed III)
					3½	18 (23 Ed III)
Walton	13	24 (4 Ed I)			18	24 (15 Ed III)
					5	36 (19 Ed III)
Stratford	4	24 (6 Ed I)				
Islip			½	32 (2 Ed II)		
Silverstone	½	12 (6 Ed I)				
Passenham	57	36 (6 Ed I)			40	18 (1 Ed III)
					30	24 (1 Ed III)
Plumpton	2½	12 (7 Ed I)	1	18 (1 Ed II)		
Rockingham	20	24 (8 Ed I)				
Weekley	8	30 (8 Ed I)				
Corby	5	36 (8 Ed I)			6	12 (9 Ed III)
Wike (nr. Hartwell)	4½	24 (9 Ed I)				
Barnwell	8	30 (9 Ed I)				
	4	14 (9 Ed I)	12	18 (15 Ed II)		
	1	12 (9 Ed I)				
Castle Ashby					15½	12 (23 Ed III)
Mears Ashby					3	24 (21 Ed III)
Dodford	7	20 (10 Ed I)				
Stoke Bruerne	30	30 (11 Ed I)				
Alderton					5½	12 (19 Ed III)
Dallington	40½	18 (12 Ed I)			10	18 (20 Ed III)
Slapton	6	24 (12 Ed I)			5	24 (20 Ed III)
Titchmarsh	30	30 (15 Ed I)	55	30 (8 Ed II)	16	24 (21 Ed III)
			50	48 (8 Ed II)		
Farndon	18	36 (16 Ed I)				
Westpery	6	24 (16 Ed I)			33¼	24 (20 Ed III)
(Paulerspury)					33¼	6 (23 Ed III)
Nassington & Yarwell	106	32 (18 Ed I)				
Yarwell					4	24 (5 Ed III)
					3	18 (7 Ed III)
Fotheringhay	280¼	36 (18 Ed I)				
Little Oakley	9	24 (18 Ed I)	6	18 (30 Ed I)	9	8 (23 Ed III)
			2	24 (16 Ed II)		
Great Oakley					½	6 (23 Ed III)
East Carlton	27	24 (18 Ed I)	10	24 (30 Ed I)	6	12 (23 Ed III)
			2	12 (16 Ed II)		
Cotton (Gretton)	10	30 (18 Ed I)			4	12 (23 Ed III)
Gt. Houghton					10	18 (13 Ed III)
					4	24 (20 Ed III)
					22¾	12 (23 Ed III)
					4	12 (24 Ed III)
					3	12 (23 Ed III)
Little Houghton	9	24 (18 Ed I)	14	32 (30 Ed I)		
Drayton	17	36 (20 Ed I)				
Chipping Warden	10	36 (20 Ed I)			12	24 (8 Ed III)
Braybrooke	4	36 (20 Ed I)				

	1st Gen.		2nd Gen.		3rd Gen.	
Halefield Lodge	3	24 (20 Ed I)	3	18 (33 Ed I)	2	10 (18 Ed III)
			1½	10 (11 Ed II)		
Finedon	3	24 (21 Ed I)	4½	60 (30 Ed I)		
	4½	24 (22 Ed I)				
Sulgrave	2	36 (22 Ed I)	5½	8 (34 Ed I)	10	16 (18 Ed III)
Thorpe	9	27 (23 Ed I)				
Greatworth	12	12 (23 Ed I)				
Pattishall	10	12 (24 Ed I)	4	24 (32 Ed I)	10	18 (10 Ed III)
					10	18 (22 Ed III)
Weedon Lois	60	24 (24 Ed I)			15	24 (17 Ed III)
Steane	18	24 (24 Ed I)				
Culworth	2	24 (24 Ed I)			6	16 (5 Ed III)
Weston	16½	24 (25 Ed I)	20	24 (15 Ed II)	19	24 (15 Ed III)
Higham Ferrers			78¾	24 (26 Ed I)	96¼	30 (1 Ed III)
Rushton			63½	24 (26 Ed I)	40	24 (1 Ed III)
Raunds			¾	30 (26 Ed I)	34¼	30 (1 Ed III)
Halse (Brackley)	100	24 (24 Ed I)	30	24 (26 Ed I)		
			30	16 (7 Ed II)		
Abington			30	36 (26 Ed I)	15	24 (23 Ed III)
Crick			3	12 (26 Ed I)	6	6 (1 Ed III)
Wakerley			25	18 (27 Ed I)	20	24 (21 Ed III)
Little Weldon			4	12 (28 Ed I)		
			4	18 (10 Ed II)		
Burton Latimer			3	12 (29 Ed I)	5	48 (1 Ed III)
			4	24 (7 Ed II)		
			6	24 (17 Ed II)		
Potterspury	12	24 (25 Ed I)	8	24 (29 Ed I)		
			8	24 (9 Ed II)		
			6	15 (18 Ed II)		
Pery (Potterspury)			8	24 (9 Ed II)		
Stoke Albany			40	24 (29 Ed I)		
Ecton			12	30 (29 Ed I)		
Welford			30	12 (29 Ed I)		
Northampton			14	60 (29 Ed I)		
Yardley Gobion			20	12 (32 Ed I)	18	24 (22 Ed III)
			18	24 (6 Ed II)		
			18	24 (6 Ed II)		
			15	4 (18 Ed II)		
			16	3 (18 Ed II)		
Evenley			6	18 (32 Ed I)		
			4	12 (9 Ed II)		
Wappenham			10	20 (32 Ed I)		
			4	12 (9 Ed II)		

TABLE II

	1st Gen.		2nd Gen.		3rd Gen.	
Norton			4	15 (32 Ed I)	5	36 (17 Ed III)
			23	36 (1 Ed II)		
Duston			30	24 (33 Ed I)	2	24 (23 Ed III)
			5	48 (1 Ed II)		
			71	36 (5 Ed II)		
Braunston			9	8 (33 Ed I)		
Milton			6	24 (33 Ed I)		
Grafton (Regis)			9	12 (33 Ed I)	2	18 (14 Ed III)
Loddington			10	12 (33 Ed I)		
			2	12 (16 Ed II)		
Watford			1	20 (10 Ed II)	20	24 (17 Ed III)
					5	24 (19 Ed III)
Chester Ho			25	24 (2 Ed II)		
Long Buckby			30	80 (4 Ed II)	10	24 (17 Ed III)
Broughton			1	24 (7 Ed II)		
Towcester			24	36 (7 Ed II)		
Astwell			6	24 (8 Ed II)		
Ashley			6	24 (15 Ed II)	2	18 (5 Ed III)
Brixsworth			43	24 (9 Ed II)		
Gretton	54	24 (2 Ed I)	4	12 (10 Ed II)	40	12 (21 Ed III)
Haselbech			10	24 (9 Ed II)		
Moor End			1	24 (9 Ed II)		
Lilford-cum-Wigsthorpe			12	24 (10 Ed II)		
Quinton			10	24 (11 Ed II)		
Moreton Pinkney			6	24 (14 Ed II)		
Torpel (Ufford)					40	6 (24 Ed III)
Harpole			5	18 (15 Ed II)	6	18 (8 Ed III)
					5	18 (12 Ed III)
					4	24 (20 Ed III)
Barton Seagrave			10	12 (15 Ed II)		
Earls Barton					12	8 (23 Ed III)
Bucknell Wood (Abthorpe)			71¼	24 (18 Ed II)		
Almer			12½	12 (18 Ed II)		
Gt. Billing			10	24 (18 Ed II)	7	6 (23 Ed III)
Grendon			20	18 (18 Ed II)	¾	12 (23 Ed III)
Wootton			11½	36 (18 Ed II)	8	24 (22 Ed III)
Denford			10	24 (19 Ed II)		
Chalcombe			32	24 (19 Ed II)		
Brampton			6	24 (19 Ed II)		
Pitesle (Pytchley)	3	24 (25 Ed I)				
Moulton	20	24 (25 Ed I)			20	24 (8 Ed III)
	20	48 (23 Ed I)			8	12 (17 Ed III)
Preston Wood					4	36 (1 Ed III)
					8	40 (9 Ed III)
Stowe					100	24 (1 Ed III)
Kislingbury					25	36 (1 Ed III)
Castor					5	24 (1 Ed III)
					5	30 (1 Ed III)

		1st Gen.		2nd Gen.		3rd Gen.
Cosgrove					2	24 (2 Ed III)
Cosgrove & Furtho					4	12 (2 Ed III)
Cosgrove & Puxley					4½	12 (2 Ed III)
					18	12 (14 Ed III)
Chelveston-cum-Caldecott					8	24 (4 Ed III)
Kings Sutton					40	24 (5 Ed III)
Fawsley					4	16 (7 Ed III)
Thorpe Mandeville					2	24 (8 Ed III)
					6	12 (8 Ed III)
Bozeat					12	18 (9 Ed III)
Deanshanger					20	24 (10 Ed III)
					10	12 (10 Ed III)
Kelmarsh					10	24 (11 Ed III)
Hardwick					¼	120 (14 Ed III)
Bradden					6	12 (17 Ed III)
Stoke & Wilbarston					62	24 (17 Ed III)
Irchester					1½	18 (19 Ed III)
Irthingborough					8	24 (9 Ed III)
Wollaston					6?	12 (20 Ed III)
Cogenhoe					16	24 (23 Ed III)
Gt. Harrowden					7	12 (23 Ed III)
RUTLAND						
Empingham	12	24 (43 H III)				
Stretton	11	10 (44 H III)	3	8 (15 Ed II)		
			7	18 (19 Ed II)		
			10½	8 (19 Ed II)		
Preston & Uppingham	19	15 (24 Ed I)				
Little Casterton			7	18 (26 Ed I)	16½	24 (10 Ed III)
			10	18 (27 Ed I)	16½	24 (18 Ed III)
Barrowden			12	30 (26 Ed I)		
			6	24 (26 Ed I)		
			24	36 (9 Ed II)		
Oakham			17	42 (28 Ed I)	17	3 (21 Ed III)
Stoke Dry			7	36 (31 Ed I)		
			3½	36 (31 Ed I)		
Haliok (Holy Oak: Leics?)			3	36 (34 Ed I)		
Ashwell			6	18 (8 Ed II)		
Barrow			4	30 (9 Ed II)		
Greetham			5	30 (9 Ed II)		
Ketton			2½	24 (16 Ed II)		
Whissendene			100	15 (18 Ed II)	20	24 (10 Ed III)
					5	18 (10 Ed III)
					2	18 (10 Ed III)
					80	24 (23 Ed III)
					16½	4 (23 Ed III)
					2	6 (23 Ed III)

TABLE II

	1st Gen.	2nd Gen.	3rd Gen.
Glaston	12	24 (20 Ed II)	
Exton		60	18 (4 Ed III)
Ryhall		15	36 (4 Ed III)
Essedine		10	24 (8 Ed III)
		10	30 (8 Ed III)
Upper Hambleton		42	24 (12 Ed III)
Market Overton		32	24 (12 Ed III)
Langham		46	48 (21 Ed III)
Seaton		7	6 (32 Ed III)

PASTURE

GENERAL REMARKS ON TABLE III

Whereas meadow was an integral part of the arable economy in the East Midlands, appearing in most extents of the Inquisitions Post Mortem, and valued high because it supported animals required for work on the arable in both winter and summer, pasture was a much more marginal resource. Pasture appeared in less than half as many entries as meadow. Furthermore, the large number of pasture values were one-half or even one-quarter the size of the more common meadow values.

At the same time the greater frequency of pasture occurrence in Beds, Bucks and Herts as against the comparatively rich meadow belt centering in Northants indicates that pasture was a more regular part of many smaller and relatively poorer estates than was meadow. The fairly consistent pasture values for these three counties over the three generations also foretells the stabilized open-field system that would resist a quick shift to enclosure for pasture. On the other hand, the distinction between pasture and meadow is a practical one that loses much of its meaning under changing conditions of agrarian organization. Thus, what was called pasture in Leicestershire, Northants, Notts and Rutland was often as valuable as meadow and the future bias towards a pastoral economy in this part of the East Midlands is already apparent. Of course, in many details in the extent this shift to pastoral activity is well documented by the third generation. At the opposite extreme, the least valuable pasture was provided by woodland, and these pastures are indicated in Table III, as in the extents, as 'parks'.

TABLE III *SUMMARY*

	ENTRIES				ACREAGE			
	Generation				Generation			
County	1st	2nd	3rd	Total	1st	2nd	3rd	Total
Beds	22	41	35	98	638	421	698	1757$^3/_4$
Bucks	31	41	29	101	385$^1/_2$	577$^1/_2$	644	1607
Herts	36	46	29	111	557	798	346	1701
Hunts	8	7	7	22	228	107$^1/_2$	121	456$^1/_2$
Leics	4	9	2	15	399	188	42	629
Northants	24	30	20	74	649	570	326	1545
Notts	1	8	4	13	2	235	67	304
Rutland	2	7	4	13	45	52	86	183
			Grand Total 447				Grand Total 8183$^1/_4$	

TABLE III — *PASTURE*

VALUE — FREQUENCY

BEDFORDSHIRE

1st Generation

Values:	1	$1\frac{1}{2}$	$1\frac{1}{3}$	3	4	6	12	16	18	24	30
Frequency:	1	1	1	1	3	3	5	1	3	2	1

2nd Generation

Values:	2	3	4	5	6	8	10	12	40
Frequency:	2	1	4	1	16	3	1	12	1

3rd Generation

Values:	2	3	4	5	6	7	8	9	12	18	24
Frequency:	1	3	3	2	12	1	4	1	4	2	1

BUCKINGHAMSHIRE

1st Generation

Values:	3	$3\frac{1}{2}$	4	5	6	8	10	12	15	17	18	24
Frequency:	1	1	1	1	9	4	2	4	2	1	1	4

2nd Generation

Values:	1	2	3	4	6	8	9	12	24	30	120
Frequency:	1	1	1	2	17	5	1	10	2	1	1

3rd Generation

Values:	1	$1\frac{1}{2}$	2	$2\frac{1}{2}$	4	6	8	9	10	12	40
Frequency:	1	2	4	1	1	6	2	1	2	7	1

TABLE III — *PASTURE*

VALUE — FREQUENCY

HERTFORDSHIRE

1st Generation

Values:	1	2	3	4	5	6	8	12	14	18
Frequency:	1	4	3	1	1	9	3	12	1	1

2nd Generation

Values:	1	$1\frac{1}{2}$	2	3	4	6	8	12	18	20	24
Frequency:	1	1	2	5	2	17	2	12	3	1	1

3rd Generation

Values:	2	4	6	8	10	12	18
Frequency:	2	3	10	5	1	6	1

HUNTINGDONSHIRE

1st Generation

Values:	6	8	10	12
Frequency:	3	2	1	2

2nd Generation

Values:	4	6	12
Frequency:	1	2	4

3rd Generation

Values:	6	8
Frequency:	5	3

TABLE III — *PASTURE*

VALUE — FREQUENCY

LEICESTERSHIRE

1st Generation

Values:	$1^1/_3$	4	18	24
Frequency:	1	1	1	1

2nd Generation

Values:	$2^1/_2$	4	10	12	24
Frequency:	1	2	1	3	2

3rd Generation

Values:	6	12
Frequency:	1	1

NORTHAMPTONSHIRE

1st Generation

Values:	3	4	6	8	10	12	24	48
Frequency:	1	1	4	4	1	8	2	2

2nd Generation

Values:	4	$4^1/_2$	6	7	8	12	16	20
Frequency:	4	1	4	1	2	9	1	1

3rd Generation

Values:	2	3	4	6	$6^1/_2$	8	10	12	24	83
Frequency:	1	1	3	4	1	1	2	5	1	1

TABLE III — *PASTURE*

VALUE — FREQUENCY

NOTTINGHAMSHIRE

1st Generation

Values:	24
Frequency:	1

2nd Generation

Values:	4	8	9	12	16	18
Frequency:	2	1	1	1	1	2

3rd Generation

Values:	12
Frequency:	4

RUTLAND

1st Generation

Values:	7	12
Frequency:	1	1

2nd Generation

Values:	1	9	10	11	12	20
Frequency:	1	1	1	1	2	1

3rd Generation

Values:	$1\frac{1}{2}$	4	$10\frac{1}{4}$	20
Frequency:	1	1	1	1

TABLE III. — *PASTURE*

	1st Gen.		2nd Gen.		3rd Gen.	
BEDFORDSHIRE						
Keysoe	8	12 (23 Ed I)	4	6 (9 Ed II?)		
	8	12 (24 Ed I)	20	6 (17 Ed II)		
Cainhoe	6	6 (15 Ed I)	3	6 (4 Ed II)	3	3 (23 Ed III)
			5	4 (12 Ed II)	1	6 (24 Ed III)
Moggerhanger	1	6 (17 Ed I)				
Kempston	6	12 (18 Ed I)			20	12 (22 Ed III)
Sutton					3	6 (9 Ed III)
Eaton Bray	2	18 (22 Ed I)	14	6 (27 Ed I)		
Aspley Guise	7	12 (23 Ed I)				
Wootton	100	12 (23 Ed I)	4	6 (17 Ed II)	7	6 (9 Ed III)
					7	6 (10 Ed III)
Flitwick	30	4 (24 Ed I)				
Westoning	15	6 (25 Ed I)	6	3 (15 Ed II)		
Campton	17	4 (25 Ed I)				
Houghton (Conquest)			9	4 (26 Ed I)		
Wymington			4	12 (26 Ed I)	$\frac{1}{2}$	12 (21 Ed III)
Higham Gobion			6	6 (29 Ed I)		
Cardington	6	24 (1286)	4	8 (30 Ed I)		
	30	1 (1280)				
Renhale	9	18 (1286)	2	12 (30 Ed I)	14	24 (9 Ed III)
			3	4 (8 Ed II)		
Warden					$\frac{1}{2}$	18 (9 Ed III)
					$1\frac{1}{2}$	8 (17 Ed III)
Biggleswade			1	12 (32 Ed I)		
Dunton (by Biggleswade)					4	9 (7 Ed III)
Odell (Little)			6	12 (32 Ed I)		
			6	40 (32 Ed I)		
Greathampstede			4	8 (2 Ed II)		
Wootton Pillinge			4	12 (2 Ed II)		
Thurleigh			4	12 (1 Ed II)		
Brogborough			3	12 (1 Ed II)		
Wreste Park			3	12 (1 Ed II)		
Stagsden					$3\frac{1}{2}$	4 (20 Ed III)
Millbrook			6	12 (4 Ed II)		
Cotes (Eastcott)	80	12 (1285)	20	6 (4 Ed II)	20	4 (7 Ed III)
Ampthill			1	6 (4 Ed II)		
Haynes			10	12 (5 Ed II)	5	6 (1 Ed III)
Stotfold			10	5 (5 Ed II)		
Willington					4	6 (1 Ed III)
Bletsoe			6	8 (6 Ed II)		
Wyboston			5	6 (10 Ed II)		
Yelden			8	12 (11 Ed II)		
Northill	2	30 (18 Ed I)	8	6 (11 Ed II)		
	120	$1\frac{1}{2}$ (18 Ed I)				

	1st Gen.		2nd Gen.		3rd Gen.	
Wilden	3½	16 (1269)	1	6 (11 Ed II)		
			6	6 (15 Ed II)		
Meppershall			4	6 (13 Ed II)	4	6 (5 Ed III)
Arlesey			3	6 (15 Ed II)		
Harrold			100	2 (17 Ed II)		
			2	12 (17 Ed II)		
Santon Barn			8	2 (17 Ed II)		
Podington			100	10 (17 Ed II)		
Toddington					101	18 (7 Ed III)
					100	5 (7 Ed III)
					80	2 (7 Ed III)
					120 (6th yr)	36 (7 Ed III)
Sudbury					4½	6 (7 Ed III)
					4	6 (8 Ed III)
Eyworth	4	4 (1282)			4	5 (8 Ed III)
Henlow					1	8 (8 Ed III)
Langford					20	12 (10 Ed III)
					20	12 (22 Ed III)
Sundon					16½	6 (12 Ed III)
					?	4 (12 Ed III)
					8	7 (12 Ed III)
					15	6 (14 Ed III)
Turvey					½	6 (14 Ed III)
					¼(Wood)	8 (14 Ed III)
Sutton					3	3 (23 Ed III)
Stevington	12	24 (1264)				
Dilwick (Stagsden)	15	18 (1286)				
	140 (park)	1⅓ (1286)				
Wood Croft (Luton)	18	3 (16 Ed I)				
Wood Croft (Luton)					3	8 (20 Ed III)
Luton			2	6 (2 Ed II)	4½	3 (2 Ed III)
			4	4 (34 Ed I)		
			2	6 (29 Ed I)		
BUCKINGHAMSHIRE						
Padbury	8	12 (22 Ed I)				
Chalfont St. Giles					4	40 (23 Ed III)
Medenham	30	? (48 H III)	8	12 (19 Ed II)	20	12 (21 Ed III)
	16	8 (15 Ed I)				
Chesham Bois	3	8 (48 H III)				
	2	6 (24 Ed I)				
Whitchurch	30	6 (48 H III)				
	12	8 (24 Ed I)				
Little Linford			2	30 (30 Ed I)		
			40 (park)	4 (30 Ed I)		
Edlesborough					2½	1½ (9 Ed III)
					2½	1 (21 Ed III)
Burnham & Eton	24	4 (56 H III?)				
Burnham					8	12 (1 Ed III)
Hitcham	10	6 (20 Ed I)				
Losmere	8	6 (20 Ed I)				
Newport Pagnell					200 (park)	2 (12 Ed III)

	1st Gen.		2nd Gen.		3rd Gen.	
Hillesden	48	6 (2 Ed I)				
	14	12 (20 Ed I)				
Tyringham	17	10 (2 Ed I)				
Astwood	5½	6 (2 Ed I)				
Wycombe	8	15 (9 Ed I)				
	20	3½ (9 Ed I)				
Buckland	2	15 (11 Ed I)			40	2 (8 Ed III)
					10	6 (8 Ed III)
Fulbrook			1	12 (33 Ed I)		
Cublington	20	12 (12 Ed I)	5	120 (33 Ed I)	10	6 (20 Ed III)
Shabbington			10	6 (6 Ed II)		
Chelmscott					4	6 (20 Ed III)
Hambleden	7	18 (13 Ed I)	24	24 (12 Ed II)	35	9 (12 Ed III)
Grendon	15	24 (13 Ed I)	3	6 (29 Ed I)	10	2½ (7 Ed III)
(Underwood)	6	6 (25 Ed I)	5	6 (32 Ed I)	23	4 (7 Ed III)
			6	12 (18 Ed II)		
Crafton	4	8 (20 Ed I)				
Lathbury	2	24 (15 Ed I)				
Gt. Missenden					19	1½ (6 Ed III)
					12	2 (11 Ed III)
Seabrook	1	6 (21 Ed I)				
Hartwell	2	6 (23 Ed I)				
Aylesbury					60	12 (12 Ed III)
Hardwick	15	24 (23 Ed I)	9	3 (3 Ed II)		
	6	17 (23 Ed I)	4	6 (4 Ed II)		
			4½	6 (9 Ed II)		
Weedon	3	24 (23 Ed I)				
Sherington			6	24 (29 Ed I)		
Chearsley	7	12 (24 Ed I)	4	12 (18 Ed II)		
Wendover & Weston Turville					3	12 (5 Ed III)
Little Broughton	16	5 (25 Ed I)				
Kingsey			4	6 (26 Ed I)		
Hanslope			93½	8 (9 Ed II)		
			40	12 (9 Ed II)		
			60	6 (18 Ed II)		
Dunton			2	9 (26 Ed I)		
Iver			2	12 (32 Ed I)	2	8 (23 Ed III)
Stoke Poges					27	10 (5 Ed III)
					30	2 (5 Ed III)
					60	(heath) ⅔ (5 Ed III)
Pitstone			20	2 (32 Ed I)		
Marsworth			5	6 (30 Ed I)		
			4	6 (35 Ed I)		
			4	6 (4 Ed II)		
Dorney			7	6 (33 Ed I)		
Stoke Goldington			6	6 (5 Ed II)		
			5	12 (2 Ed II)		
Stewkley			2	6 (35 Ed I)		
East Claydon	24	10 (25 Ed I)	3	6 (6 Ed II)		

	1st Gen.		2nd Gen.		3rd Gen.	
Easington			2½	8 (35 Ed I)		
			12	6 (3 Ed II)		
Gt. Marlow			20	8 (35 Ed I)		
Marlow			16	8 (8 Ed II)		
			100	1 (8 Ed II)		
La Waterhall			12	12 (1 Ed II)		
Eton			8	8 (1 Ed II)		
Eythorpe			3	12 (2 Ed II)		
Worminghall			4	4 (8 Ed II)		
Workington (Waddesdon?)			1	6 (17 Ed II)		
Simpson			7	6 (17 Ed II)		
Stantonbury			3	12 (19 Ed II)		
Aston Bernard (Mullins)					4	12 (3 Ed III)
Calverton					4	8 (5 Ed III)
Gt. & Little Kimble					3	12 (5 Ed III)
Chenies (Isenhampsted)					24	6 (9 Ed III)
Preston					2	6 (12 Ed III)
					1	12 (17 Ed III)
Wolverton					12	10 (15 Ed III)
					12	6 (23 Ed III)
HERTFORDSHIRE						
Hunsdon	6	6 (25 Ed I)				
Sacombe	5	6 (37 H III)	10	12 (8 Ed II)	4	18 (7 Ed III)
	5½	6 (11 Ed I)	11	8 (14 Ed II)		
	2	3 (11 Ed I)				
	5	12 (17 Ed I)				
Standon	9½	12 (46 H III)	18	12 (35 Ed I)	8	12 (15 Ed III)
	140	3 (46 H III)	16	6 (1 Ed II)		
	12½	12 (24 Ed I)	5	12 (8 Ed II)		
			20	12 (8 Ed II)		
Albury	4	12 (55 H III)	6	3 (34 Ed I)		
Flamstead			3	4 (3 Ed II)	3	4 (11 Ed III)
Hitchin	18	6 (53 H III)				
Hemel Hempstead			4	6 (30 Ed I)		
			43	3 (30 Ed I)		
Sawbridgeworth	9¼	14 (56 H III)	3	18 (4 Ed II)		
	30 (park)	6 (56 H III)	12	20 (15 Ed II)		
	40 (park)	3 (23 Ed I)	20	4 (15 Ed II)		
	20	2 (23 Ed I)				
	12	18 (23 Ed I)				
Pishobury	20	12 (22 Ed I)				
Broxbourne	10	4 (? Ed I)				
Little Berkhamsted	20	2 (23 Ed I)	40 (park)	2 (3 Ed II)	15	2 (11 Ed III)
			15	2 (19 Ed II)	40 (park)	2 (11 Ed III)
Berkhamsted	4	6 (56 H III)	18	12 (32? Ed I)		
Offley					4	8 (9 Ed III)
					26	4 (9 Ed III)
					7	6 (23 Ed III)

	1st Gen.		2nd Gen.		3rd Gen.	
Gt. Wymondley	3	12 [11 Ed I]	4	12 (12 Ed II)		
Wyddial	17	12 (12 Ed I)			5	6 (15 Ed III)
					4	12 (15 Ed III)
Gt. Gaddesden			6	6 (7 Ed II)		
Gaddesden			$21\frac{1}{4}$	6 (15 Ed II)		
			24	8 (15 Ed II)		
Wigginton			5	3 (33 Ed I)		
Betlow	4	6 (13 Ed I)				
Ware	$12\frac{1}{4}$	12 (12 Ed I)				
King's Walden	6	6 (14 Ed I)	8	12 (7 Ed II)	10	12 (3 Ed III)
	2	12 (6 Ed I)				
Little Hormead			3	12 (7 Ed II)		
Hormead	8	12 (24 Ed I)				
	5	5 (14 Ed I)				
Watton at Stone	8	8 (14 Ed I)	6	6 (16 Ed II)	8	6 (3 Ed III)
Patmore Hall	3	12 (14 Ed I)				
Gt. & Little Munden			6	6 (30 Ed I)		
			40 (park)	6 (30 Ed I)		
Furneux Pelham	6	8 (21 Ed I)				
Thundridge	40	2 (21 Ed I)				
	20	2 (22 Ed I)				
Thorley	8	8 (22 Ed I)				
Pirton	10	1 (23 Ed I)	12	6 (33 Ed I)	5	12 (21 Ed III)
			4	3 (18 Ed II)		
Theobald St. (Oldenham)	6	6 (24 Ed I)				
Pope's Hall (Buckland)	8	12 (24 Ed I)	8	12 (8 Ed II)		
Eastwick			4	6 (29 Ed I)	20	12 (15 Ed III)
(atte Flore)			38	18 (24 Ed II)		
Bengeo			6	24 (32 Ed I)		
Bishops Hatfield			5	12 (1 Ed II)		
			60 (park)	$1\frac{1}{2}$ (18 Ed II)		
Bishey (Wood)					24	6 (4 Ed III)
Hatfield					2	6 (1 Ed III)
					$2\frac{1}{2}$	6 (1 Ed III)
Hertingfordbury			12	6 (18 Ed II)		
			80 (park)	$\frac{3}{4}$ (18 Ed II)		
Great Anstey			2	12 (7 Ed II)		
Little Anstey			2	12 (7 Ed II)		
Westreed			4	6 (8 Ed II)		
Reed					4	6 (15 Ed III)
Willian					$1\frac{1}{2}$	8 (23 Ed III)
Berwick			2	18 (12 Ed II)		
Shenley			40 (park)	3 (12 Ed II)		
Thele (Stanstead St. Margarets)			3	6 (12 Ed II)		
Hoddesdon			120	1 (16 Ed II)		
Holwell			8	6 (17 Ed II)		
Little Holwell			$3\frac{1}{2}$	6 (18 Ed II)	2	6 (1 Ed III)
Twendesbury			6	6 (18 Ed II)		
Essendon			6	6 (18 Ed II?)		
Bayford			5	6 (18 Ed II?)		

	1st Gen.		2nd Gen.		3rd Gen.	
Cheshunt					3	4 (9 Ed III)
					40 (park)	2 (9 Ed III)
Knebworth					20	10 (9 Ed III)
Nuthampstead					46	6 (10 Ed III)
					6	8 (10 Ed III)
Plessis					12	6 (12 Ed III)
Mardleybury					8	8 (12 Ed III)
Therfield					5	8 (14 Ed III)
Welles (Wellbury Ho: Offley)					11	12 (15 Ed III)
HUNTINGDONSHIRE						
Dillington	10	6 (25 Ed I)				
Hamerton	2	12 (2 Ed I)				
Southoe	2	6 (2 Ed I)				
Lymage					6	8 (23 Ed III)
Brampton			42	12 (6 Ed II)	25	6 (9 Ed III)
					64	8 (23 Ed III)
Washingley	3	8 (16 Ed I)				
Everton (Beds)	3	6 (22 Ed I)			12	6 (5 Ed III)
Fen Stanton &	140 (marsh)	12 (23 Ed I)	52 (marsh)	4 (19 Ed II)		
Hilton	$24\frac{1}{2}$	10 (23 Ed I)				
Gt Staughton	44	8 (24 Ed I)				
Upton			$\frac{1}{2}$	12 (26 Ed I)		
Ellington Thorpe					6	6 (23 Ed III)
Caldecote (?)			2	12 (32 Ed I)	$2\frac{1}{2}$	6 (4 Ed III)
					1	6 (5 Ed III)
Hemingford (Grey)			5	12 (1 Ed II)		
Toseland			4	6 (17 Ed II)		
Little Paxton			2	6 (16 Ed II)		
Offord Darcy					5	8 (5 Ed III)
LEICESTERSHIRE						
Mountsorrel	9	4 (39 H III)				
Evington	20	18 (56 H III)				
Barrow-upon-Soar			10	24 (1 Ed II)		
			360 (park)	$1\frac{1}{3}$ (1 Ed II)		
Foston			4	12 (8 Ed II)		
Willoughby Waterless			1	12 (29 Ed I)		
Medbourne			28	24 (30 Ed I)		
Ab Kettleby			$\frac{1}{2}$	24 (31 Ed I)		
Lobthorpe (Lincs)			30	10 (32 Ed I)		
Cotesbach			5	4 (3 Ed III)		
Donington			96	12 (4 Ed II)		
Seagrave			$20\frac{1}{2}$	$2\frac{1}{2}$ (19 Ed II)		
Castle Donington					40	6 (4 Ed III)
Newton Harcourt					2	12 (6 Ed III)
Barkestone			3	4 (8 Ed II)		

	1st Gen.		2nd Gen.		3rd Gen.	
NORTHAMPTONSHIRE						
Rothwell	59	12 (47? H III)	30	8 (35 Ed I)		
	10½	8 (47 H III)				
	72¾	4/5 (24 Ed I)				
Wadenhoe	10	6 (18 H III)				
Faxton	35	4 (50 H III)				
Easton (on-the-Hill)			18	18 (26 Ed I)		
Whitfield	6	12 (22 Ed I)				
Naseby	54½	8 (22 Ed I)	16	3 (35 Ed I)		
	54	10 (24 Ed I)	40	2 (35 Ed I)		
Harringworth			7	12 (16 Ed II)		
Gretton	20	12 (2 Ed I)				
Torpel					60 (park)	4 (4 Ed III)
Upton			2	12 (8 Ed II)		
Cotterstock	7½	48 (18 Ed I)	9	4½ (30 Ed I)		
Walton					2	12 (5 Ed III)
Passenham	32	12 (6 Ed I)				
Plumpton			3	4 (1 Ed II)		
Corby	12	6 (8 Ed I)				
Castle Ashby					10	6 (23 Ed III)
Mears Ashby	7	48 (10 Ed I)				
Alderton					5	4 (19 Ed III)
Titchmarsh	10	12 (15 Ed I)				
Westpery (Paulerspury)	30	24 (16 Ed I)				
Yarwell					46	10 (5 Ed III)
					49	83 (7 Ed III)
Fotheringhay	92½	3 (18 Ed I)				
Little Oakley	2	6 (18 Ed I)				
Gt. Houghton					1½	10 (20 Ed III)
Drayton	10	24 (20 Ed I)				
Finedon	2	12 (21 Ed I)				
	1	12 (22 Ed I)				
Thorpe					4	12 (17 Ed III)
Pattishall	6	8 (24 Ed I)	3	16 (32 Ed I)		
Weedon Lois	80	6 (24 Ed I)			4	12 (17 Ed III)
Weston	15	12 (25 Ed I)				
Higham Ferrers					24½	24 (1 Ed III)
Raunds			6¼	12 (26 Ed I)		
Wakerley					10	12 (21 Ed III)
Burton Latimer			4	4½ (29 Ed I)		
Potterspury			2	12 (9 Ed II)		
Pery (Potterspury)			2	12 (9 Ed II)		
Stoke Albany			4	12 (29 Ed I)		
Yardley Gobion			20	4 (6 Ed II)	28	6 (22 Ed III)
Evenley			3	6 (32 Ed I)		
			3	6 (9 Ed II)		
Wappenham			6	20 (32 Ed I)		
			8	4 (9 Ed II)		
East Haddon			6	12 (33 Ed I)		
Duston			12	12 (5 Ed II)		

	1st Gen.		2nd Gen.		3rd Gen.	
Loddington			4	6 (16 Ed II)		
Towcester			10	12 (7 Ed II)		
Lilford-cum-Wigsthorpe			12	6 (10 Ed II)		
Grendon			10	12 (18 Ed II)		
Wootton			6	7 (18 Ed II)	4	3 (22 Ed III)
Moulton	20	8 (25 Ed I)			4	8 (17 Ed III)
Kings Sutton					12	6 (5 Ed III)
Deanshanger					3	6½ (10 Ed III)
Cosgrove					12	2 (14 Ed III)
Stoke and Wilbarston					40	6 (17 Ed III)
Irchester					4	4 (19 Ed III)
Norton					3	12 (17 Ed III)
Sulgrave			2	4 (34 Ed I)		
NOTTINGHAMSHIRE						
Bridgeford			2	24 (1297)		
Langar			15	4 (1298)	20 (park)	12 (1328)
			15	4 (1314)		
East & West Leake			5 (park)	12 (1323)		
			4	16 (1323)		
Staunton-in-the-Vale			24 (park)	8 (1326)		
Eaton			16 (park)	9 (1326)		
Egmanton			140 (park)	18 (1326)		
Bunny			16 (park)	18 (1326)		
Ratcliffe on Trent					3 (park)	12 (1329)
Clifton					20 (park)	12 (1327)
Clifton (Wylford)					24 (park)	12 (1327)
RUTLAND						
Preston &	5	12 (24 Ed I)				
Uppingham	40	7 (24 Ed I)				
Barrowden			4	9 (26 Ed I)		
			6	10 (9 Ed II)		
Casterton			32	1 (27 Ed I)		
Oakham			4	20 (28 Ed I)	4	10¼ (21 Ed III)
					4	20 (21 Ed III)
Stoke Dry			2	12 (31 Ed I)		
			2	11 (31 Ed I)		
Ashwell			3	12 (8 Ed II)		
Market Overton					36	4 (12 Ed III)
Langham					42½	12 (21 Ed III)

WOOD

GENERAL REMARKS ON TABLE IV

Wood was reported in the Inquisitions Post Mortem for only one-half as many entries as pasture, so that it is correspondingly more difficult to assess general patterns of value for the whole of the East Midlands. This may be explained in large part by the fact that for the heart of the royal forest areas little is reported on wood by these Inquisitions. There are no entries for Notts, none until the third generation for Rutland, only three (over two generations) for Leicestershire, and only 21 over the whole period for Northants. Of ancient forest regions, only those forest areas of Bucks and Hunts are fairly well represented. On the other hand, for Beds, Bucks and Herts as a whole there are a good number of references to wood, so that sufficient evidence is available to indicate the value of wood for the 'ordinary' arable economy of the East Midlands. Again, however, this does not suggest that regional patterns can be seen since, unlike meadow and pasture, there are considerable variations in amounts of wood from quite large to the many small. For Hunts more particularly larger woods do tend to appear with larger estates.

Uses of the wood indicated by the Inquisitions fall into four categories: regular pasture, intermittent pasture, normal domestic uses (underwood: *subbosc'*) and sale of timber. Many of the regular pasture uses have been included under Table III as 'park'. Further use of wood as pasture is indicated by the similar pasture values given to many of these acres in Table IV, although the many very small values indicated how marginal their pasture resources were. Underwood was more valuable, but not regularly available every year, as may be seen by the relatively small actual amounts of wood (in brackets) valued, or the fact that wood was only available for this purpose every third, fourth or more often sixth or seventh year. The fourth category of woodland use, that is sale of timber and assarting of the land, is well explained in the 1274 entry for Eaton Bray, Beds. On this estate, one 28 acre unit of wood could have the timber sold for 30 shillings per acre and could be asserted at 9 pence per acre; the 115 acre wood on the same estate was assessed as follows: 10

acres could be cleared for 50 shillings per acre for the wood, 96 acres for 40 shillings per acre for the wood, 9 acres had wood that was worth only two shillings per acre if cleared and the same 9 acres was worth two shillings for pasture if not assarted. The 3 acres of wood at Sawbridgeworth, Herts, valued at 24 shillings was likely also a valuation for timber since the 8 acres of underwood in the same village was worth only 8 shillings.

TABLE IV — *SUMMARY*

	ENTRIES				ACREAGE			
	Generation				Generation			
County	1st	2nd	3rd	Total	1st	2nd	3rd	Total
Beds	17	19	12	48	1303	897	352	2552
Bucks	12	20	21	53	625	945	448	2018
Herts	29	43	15	87	984	1905	384	3273
Hunts	10	15	6	31	326	484	142	952
Leics	1	2	—	3	1200	103	—	1303
Northants	5	9	7	21	148	256	138	542
Notts	—	—	—	—	—	—	—	—
Rutland	—	3	—	3	—	58	—	58
			Grand Total 246				Grand Total 10,698	

TABLE IV — *WOOD*

VALUE — FREQUENCY

BEDFORDSHIRE

1st Generation

Values:	1/2	1 1/5	1/3	2	2 1/2	2 2/3	5	6	36	48	80	360
Frequency:	1	1	1	1	1	2	1	3	1	1	2	1

2nd Generation

Values:	1	2	2 2/3	4	5	6	12	16	24	48	60	72
Frequency:	1	1	2	2	1	3	2	1	2	1	1	1

3rd Generation

Values:	1 1/2	3 1/2	5	6	18	20	24	26	36	60
Frequency:	1	1	1	2	1	1	1	1	2	1

BUCKINGHAMSHIRE

1st Generation

Values:	1/3	1/2	3/4	1 1/2	2	3	4	5	6	10	13
Frequency:	1	2	1	1	1	1	1	1	1	1	1

2nd Generation

Values:	4/5	2/3	1/4	1/2	1	1 1/2	2	2 1/2	3	3 1/4	4	4 1/2	6	24
Frequency:	1	1	1	1	3	1	1	2	3	1	2	1	2	1

3rd Generation

Values:	1	1 1/2	2	2 1/2	4	5	6	9	20	48
Frequency:	6	1	1	1	3	1	2	1	1	1

TABLE IV — *WOOD*

VALUE — FREQUENCY

HERTFORDSHIRE

1st Generation

Values:	3/4	1	1 1/2	2	2 2/3	3	4	5	6	7	12	24	96
Frequency:	1	2	1	3	1	1	9	1	4	2	1	1	2

2nd Generation

Values:	1/2	3/4	4/5	1	1 1/3	1 1/2	2	2 1/2	3	4	5	6	8	10
Frequency:	2	1	2	2	1	2	6	2	6	7	2	7	1	1

3rd Generation

Values:	4/5	1	2	3	4	6	8	12	36	40
Frequency:	1	3	3	2	1	1	1	1	1	1

HUNTINGDONSHIRE

1st Generation

Values:	1	1 1/2	2 4/5	4	5	6	12	60
Frequency:	2	1	1	1	2	1	1	1

2nd Generation

Values:	1/3	2 1/5	3	4	5	6	8	12	18	24	36
Frequency:	1	1	3	1	1	3	1	1	1	1	1

3rd Generation

Values:	2/5	3	4	11	12
Frequency:	1	2	1	1	1

TABLE IV — *WOOD*

VALUE — FREQUENCY

LEICESTERSHIRE

1st Generation

Values:	$\frac{2}{5}$
Frequency:	1

2nd Generation

Values:	3	8
Frequency:	1	1

NORTHAMPTONSHIRE

1st Generation

Values:	$\frac{4}{5}$	2	3	7	12
Frequency:	1	1	1	1	1

2nd Generation

Values:	1	$2\frac{1}{2}$	3	5	6	8	$9\frac{1}{2}$
Frequency:	1	1	1	1	3	1	1

3rd Generation

Values:	1	2	$3\frac{1}{2}$	12
Frequency:	1	4	1	1

RUTLAND

3rd Generation only

Values:	$2\frac{1}{2}$	4	5
Frequency:	1	1	1

TABLE IV. — *WOOD*

	1st Gen.		2nd Gen.		3rd Gen.	
BEDFORDSHIRE						
Keysoe	220 (16)	80 (23 Ed I)	60	$2\frac{2}{3}$ (9 Ed II?)		
	220 (16)	80 (24 Ed I)	180 (20)	24 (17 Ed II)		
Cainhoe			80	2 (4 Ed II)	40 (6)	24 (24 Ed III)
			40	1 (19 Ed II)	40 (6)	20 (24 Ed III)
Moggerhanger	30	$2\frac{2}{3}$ (17 Ed I)				
Kempston					30	$3\frac{1}{2}$ (22 Ed III)
Chanston (Roxton)	13	2 (18 Ed I)				
Shelton	16	5 (20 Ed I)				
Staploe	3	6 (20 Ed I)				
Aspley Guise	80	$\frac{1}{2}$ (23 Ed I)				
Wootton	182 (20)	36 (23 Ed I)	10 (2)	24 (17 Ed II)	20 (3)	18 (8 Ed III)
					7 (6th yr)	5 (9 Ed III)
Westoning			6	12 (15 Ed II)		
Houghton (Conquest)	30	$2\frac{2}{3}$ (26 Ed I)				
Luton	10	$1\frac{1}{5}$ (27 Ed I)			3	6 (4 Ed III)
Streatley			10	6 (29 Ed I)		
Higham Gobion			21 (3rd yr)	6 (29 Ed I)		
Cardington	203	6 (1286)	140	5 (30 Ed I)		
			72	4 (8 Ed II)		
Renhale	$2\frac{1}{2}$	$2\frac{1}{2}$ (1286)	5	16 (8 Ed II)		
Warden (Gravenhurst)	16	$\frac{1}{3}$ (9 Ed I)				
Greathampstede			2	4 (2 Ed II)		
Wootton Pillinge			[$15\frac{3}{4}$]	48 (2 Ed II)		
Cotes (Eastcott)	120	6 (1285)			60 (6th yr)	36 (7 Ed III)
Willington					100	$1\frac{1}{2}$ (1 Ed III)
Bletsoe			20	12 (6 Ed II)		
Northill			60	$2\frac{2}{3}$ (11 Ed II)		
Wilden			6	6 (15 Ed II)		
Meppershall					10	6 (5 Ed III)
Harrold			140 (20)	60 (17 Ed II)		
Santon Barn			6 (1)	72 (17 Ed II)		
Podington			24 (3)	60 (17 Ed II)		
Shillington					10	26 (6 Ed III)
Sudbury					20 (3)	36 (8 Ed III)
Stevington					12 (7 th yr)	60 (23 Ed III)
		(360)				
Eaton Bray		28 (or) (1274)				
		(9)				
		115 (10-600) (1274)				
		(96-480)				
		(9-24)				
Stagsden	15 (3)	48 (1283)				

	1st Gen.		2nd Gen.		3rd Gen.	
BUCKINGHAMSHIRE						
Chalfont	52	6 (32 H III)				
Medenham	120	$^{3}/_{4}$ (48 H III)	25	1 (19 Ed II)		
Chesham Bois	10	$^{1}/_{2}$ (48 H III)			4	20 (13 H III)
Little Lindford			40	3 (19 Ed II)	40	$2^{1}/_{2}$ (12 Ed III)
Edlesborough			16	$1^{1}/_{2}$ (32 Ed II)	10	1 (8 Ed III)
Cippenham	20	4 (56 H III)				
Burnham					8	5 (1 Ed III)
					6	4 (1 Ed III)
Hitcham & Losmere					40	1 (12 Ed III)
Wavendon					27 (7 th yr)	1 (7 Ed III)
Haversham					27	$1^{1}/_{2}$ (21 Ed III)
Linslade	6	3 (3 Ed III?)				
Linslade & Southcott	3	2 (14 Ed I)				
Gt. Leckhampstead	6	10 (8 Ed I)				
Wycombe	60	$^{1}/_{3}$ (9 Ed I)				
Shabbington			200	$^{1}/_{4}$ (6 Ed II)		
Hambleden			16	$2^{1}/_{2}$ (12 Ed II)	35	2 (12 Ed III)
Little Missenden	6	13 (33 H III)			48	1 (6 Ed III)
Missenden	144	$^{1}/_{2}$ (18 Ed. I)			12	1 (11 Ed III)
Gt. Missenden			15	4 (29 Ed I)		
Little Brickhill	100	$1^{1}/_{2}$ (24 Ed I)				
Hanslope			160	1? (18 Ed II)		
			40	$4^{1}/_{2}$ (18 Ed II)		
Pitstone			4	3 (32 Ed I)		
Woburn			5	6 (29 Ed I)		
Dorney			40	$^{1}/_{2}$ (33 Ed I)		
Stoke Goldington					40	1 (23 Ed III)
					20	4 (23 Ed III)
Stewkley			8	3 (35 Ed I)		
Farnham			60	$^{2}/_{3}$ (3 Ed II)		
			20	$^{4}/_{5}$ (10 Ed II)		
Holmer Green					14	9 (9 Ed III)
Emberton					4 (7 th yr)	48 (5 Ed III)
Dinton			5	2 (7 Ed II)		
Chilton			168	6 (9 Ed II)		
Simpson			10 (2)	24 (17 Ed II)		
Stantonbury			3	4 (18 Ed II)		
Hardmead			10	$2^{1}/_{2}$ (19 Ed II)		
Penn			100	$3^{1}/_{4}$+ (19 Ed II)		
East Claydon	100	5 (25 Ed I)				
Salden					6	4 (5 Ed III)
Foscott					4	6 (7 Ed III)
Chenies					20	— (9 Ed III)
(Isenhampstead)					60	— (9 Ed III)
Preston					11 (2)	— (12 Ed III)
Shenley					12	6 (15 Ed III)

TABLE IV

	1st Gen.			2nd Gen.			3rd Gen.	
HERTFORDSHIRE								
Hunsdon	40	1	(25 Ed I)					
Sacombe	8	1	(17 Ed I)	20	4	(8 Ed II)	15 (3)	36 (7 Ed III)
				18	1	(14 Ed II)		
Standon				10	$2\frac{1}{2}$	(8 Ed II)	12	3 (15 Ed III)
				20	6	(8 Ed II)		
Meesden	18	7	(47 H III)	14	6	(7 Ed II)		
Albury	13	12	(47 H III)					
	12	2	(55 H III)					
Flamstead				4	6	(32 Ed I)		
Berkhamsted	200	6	(56 H III)	120	4	(32 Ed I)		
Hemel Hempstead	200	6	(56 H III)	30	1	(30 Ed I)		
Sawbridgeworth	3	96	(56 H III)					
	4	96	(56 H III)					
Pishobury	100	4	(22 Ed I)					
Marlin Farm	20	24	(3 Ed I)					
(Northchurch)				5	5	(35 Ed I)		
Little Berkhamsted	24	4	(23 Ed I)	3	2	(3 Ed II)		
				40	6	(9 Ed II)		
Offley	30	3	(20 Ed I)	30	$1\frac{1}{2}$	(2 Ed II)	10	2 (9 Ed III)
				41	2	(20 Ed II)	42	40 (9 Ed III)
Walkern				208	5	(6 Ed II)		
				$16\frac{1}{4}$	2	(6 Ed II)		
Little Wymondley				12	6	(12 Ed II)		
Gaddesden	40	$1\frac{1}{2}$	(12 Ed I)	117	6	(15 Ed II)		
	3	2	(20 Ed I)					
Walden, Kings &	20	4	(14 Ed I)	40	4	(7 Ed II)	70	4 (3 Ed III)
St. Pauls	23	4	(14 Ed I)					
	2	6	(6 Ed I)					
Hormead	20	4	(24 Ed I)					
	61	2	(14 Ed I)					
Watton at Stone				20	4	(16 Ed II)	6	2 (3 Ed III)
Patmore Hall	60	$\frac{3}{4}$	(14 Ed I)					
Furneux Pelham	3	6	(21 Ed I)					
	4	7	(21 Ed I)					
Thundridge	30	4	(21 Ed I)					
	15	4	(22 Ed I)					
Thorley	5	$2\frac{2}{3}$	(22 Ed I)					
Pirton	10	4	(23 Ed I)	12	2	(33 Ed I)		
Theobald St. (Oldenham)	12	5	(24 Ed I)	4	3	(27 Ed I)		
Chelsing	4	4	(24 Ed I)					
Pope's Hall (Buckland)				6	4	(8 Ed II)		
Gt. & Little Munden				60	$1\frac{1}{3}$	(27 Ed I)		
				20	3	(27 Ed I)		
				80	3	(6 Ed II)		
Stocks				8	$\frac{3}{4}$	(27 Ed I)		
Eastwick (atte Flore)							30	12 (15 Ed III)

	1st Gen.		2nd Gen.		3rd Gen.	
Eastwick			2	3 (29 Ed I)		
			80	3 (11 Ed II)		
Almshoe			12	2 (32 Ed I)		
Lilley			15	8 (9 Ed II)	20	6 (7 Ed III)
Bishops Hatfield			100	$^{4}/_{5}$ (32 Ed I)		
			4	$^{1}/_{2}$ (32 Ed I)		
			20	4 (1 Ed II)		
Great Bishey Wood (Wheathampstead)			10	$2^{1}/_{2}$ (34 Ed I)		
Kings Langley			4	3 (32 Ed I)		
Hertingfordbury			50	5 (3 Ed II)		
Thele (Stanstead St. Margarets)			8	10 (12 Ed II)		
Walhamstede (Hitchin) & Redbourn			60	4 (15 Ed II)		
Hoddesdon			120	$^{3}/_{4}$ (16 Ed II)		
Bennington			300 (deer)	$^{4}/_{5}$ (17 Ed II)		
			88	$1^{1}/_{2}$ (17 Ed II)		
Little Holwell			8	6 (18 Ed II)	3	2 (1 Ed III)
Twendesbury			60	$^{1}/_{2}$ (18 Ed II)		
Bayford			6	2 (18 Ed II?)	2	3 (19 Ed III)
Westwick Hall by St Albans					22	1 (3 Ed III)
Knebworth					50	1 (9 Ed III)
Plessis					40	1 (12 Ed III)
Buckland					12	8 (12 Ed III)
Mardleybury					50	$^{4}/_{5}$ (12 Ed III)

HUNTINGDONSHIRE

	1st Gen.		2nd Gen.		3rd Gen.	
Grafham			3	6 (7 Ed II)		
Dillington	7	60 (56 H III)	2	6 (16 Ed II)		
	80	$1^{1}/_{2}$ (25 Ed I)				
Hamerton	16	5 (10 Ed I)	8	12 (4 th yr) (18 Ed II)		
Southoe	4	6 (2 Ed I)	4	6 (35 Ed I)		
	12	1 (2 Ed I)				
Southoe & Orton Waterville					4	12 (13 Ed III)
Lymage					60	11 (23 Ed III)
Brampton			100	$^{1}/_{3}$ (6 Ed II)	60	$^{2}/_{5}$ (9 Ed III)
Washingley	9	5 (16 Ed I)				
	10	12 (16 Ed I)				
Diddington	80	1 (18 Ed I)				
Everton (Beds)	8	4 (22 Ed I)	140 (20)	24 (15 Ed II)		
Alconbury & Weston			80 (10)	8 (19 Ed II)		
Gt. Staughton	100	$2^{4}/_{2}$ (24 Ed I)	100	$2^{2}/_{5}$ (26 Ed I)		
Upton			2	3 (26 Ed I)		
Ellington Thorpe			4	4 (26 Ed I)	16	4 (23 Ed III)

TABLE IV

	1st Gen.			2nd Gen.			3rd Gen.		
Glatton				12	3	(28 Ed I)			
Caldecote (?)							8	3	(4 Ed III)
							4	3	(5 Ed III)
Yelling and Hemingford Turberville				6 (6th yr)	36	(17 Ed II)			
Yelling				5	5	(1 Ed II)			
Toseland				6 (6th yr)	18	(17 Ed II)			
Great Gransden				12	3	(8 Ed II)			
LEICESTERSHIRE									
Barrow-upon-Soar	1200	⅖	(1 Ed I)						
Kirby Ballards				3	8	(31 Ed I)			
Lobthorpe (Lincs)				100	3	(32 Ed I)			
NORTHAMPTONSHIRE									
Rothwell	10	12	(24 Ed I)	40	6	(35 Ed I)			
Faxton	24	7	(50 H III)						
Passenham	2	3	(6 Ed I)						
Rockingham	100	⅘	(8 Ed I)						
Castle Ashby							40	2	(23 Ed III)
Mears Ashby				6	6	(18 Ed II)			
Westpery (Paulerspury)							42	2	(23 Ed III)
Little Oakley							10	3½	(23 Ed III)
East Carlton	12	2	(18 Ed I)						
Wakerley				15	5	(27 Ed I)	10	12	(21 Ed III)
Wilby				3	8	(28 Ed I)			
Little Weldon				60	1	(28 Ed I)			
Norton				4	3	(32 Ed I)			
Milton				30	9½	(33 Ed I)			
Grafton (Regis)				100	2½	(33 Ed I)			
Cosgrove & Furtho							12	2	(2 Ed III)
Cosgrove & Puxley							12	2	(2 Ed III)
Cosgrove							12	1	(14 Ed III)
Doddington (Gt.)				1	6	(34 Ed I)			
RUTLAND									
Casterton				31	2½	(27 Ed I)			
Stoke Dry				12	4	(31 Ed I)			
Uppingham				15	5	(31 Ed I)			

STUDY II

THE END OF ASSARTING IN SOME ROYAL FORESTS OF THE EAST MIDLANDS

GENERAL OBSERVATIONS

It is a commonplace of English economic history that closing of the forest frontier in the thirteenth century marked the end of an era of economic growth, perhaps as significantly for many regions as the closing of the American frontier in the nineteenth century in Frederick Jackson Turner's famous theory.[1] And yet, studies of the detail of forest clearing or assarting, to say nothing of the social significance of this phenomenon, have been negligible. The reason for this appears to have been the predominant concern of historians with the massive central fact of the royal forests as a feature of legal and constitutional history.[2] Only by the 1960's were historians showing signs of

1 Cf. especially, *The Frontier in American History*, N. Y., 1921.

2 The Oxford Histories may be cited in illustration: A. L. Poole in the twelfth-century volume introduces his treatment of the forests with the remark, "In the intervals between battle and business the feudal aristocracy followed the hounds", and continues in this vein for several pages, merely throwing in as an aside at one point, "Besides judicial fines there were considerable rents accruing from pasturage and from assarts or clearings made in the forest for agricultural purposes" (p. 34). One finds no explicit reference whatsoever to assarts in the thirteenth-century volume of Sir Maurice Powicke or the fourteenth-century study of May McKisack, although there are thorough analyses of forest perambulations and the significance of these for disafforestment. (cf. *The Fourteenth Century* 1307-1399, Oxford, 1959, p. 207: "In the fourteenth century, however, its (forest law) security was somewhat relaxed; and the long struggle for disafforestment comes to an end in 1327, when, probably as a bid for popularity, Isabella and Mortimer sponsored an act which ordered that the perambulations made under Edward I should be taken as establishing the future boundaries of the forest...")

As might be expected from the nature of their agrarian intersts, economic historians have been more concerned with the question of assarting. Nellie Neilson, for instance, drew attention to the valuable materials in the Forest Proceedings (PRO) in her chapter for Willard's *English Government at Work*. And, in the *Cambridge Economic History* (1941) she stated: "Another aspect of the history of the waste, assarting, has not received the study it deserves." (p. 458) But she considerably neutralized the force of this challenge by then drawing the reader back into traditional historiography: "The lesser emphasis on assarting in England was no doubt due in part to its being smaller in extent than in some continental countries, but also in part to the existence in England of great royal forests..." (459)

shifting from the older historiography, most noteworthy perhaps being the work now under way by the economic historians[3] and historical geographers.[4]

What has emerged from these new studies is an awareness of the immense task still awaiting the mediaeval historian. As always, the most exigent first service to be performed by the mediaevalist is to make available data lying hidden beneath literary remains, data that are so often difficult of access and interpretation. Since G. J. Turner has edited the basic formulary, and it is impossible to envisage the full editing of these records, two stages of study seem to be indicated. Much remains for the social and economic historian in the Royal Forest Proceedings that survive for many parts of the country. The most obvious first stage, therefore, is the extraction of data pertaining to land, sowing, values, etc. from these Forest Proceedings. This is the main purpose of the following study. The second stage is to pursue on the regional and local level the personal detail concerning actual tenants and the specific detail about location of assarts, detail that can only be fully extracted by the use of local records.[5]

3 In the second edition of *The Agrarian Life in the Middle Ages (Cambridge Economic History of Europe*, II, 1966), Professor Postan bluntly dismissed traditional historiography by shifting emphasis from hunting and sport to economics of the forest (p. 551). Unfortunately, the radical implications of Postan's statement have had little impact, perhaps due to the inevitably general scope allowed his remarks, and above all to the fact that the reader searches in vain in the bibliography for further leads. The considerable possibilities of detailed work on the local level may be seen in the unpublished thesis of J. Z. Titow, "Land and Population on the Bishop of Winchester's Estates, 1209-1350" (University of Cambridge, Ph. D., 1962).

4 Colin Tubbs on the New Forest, Helen Boulton on Sherwood, Peter Brandon on the Sussex Weald and B. K. Roberts on the forest of Arden are examples of a list that might extend to a score of names.

5 One could cite in illustration the unpublished Birmingham thesis of John West, *The Administration and Economy of the Forest of Feckenham during the Early Middle Ages.* This thesis did two things worthy of special note. First, it recognized that traditional historiography virtually excluded the possibility for study of forest economy and society. One would wonder how peasants survived in the forest at all, West exclaims (p. 19).

Secondly, this thesis studied the life of the forest people from within. Manors and villagers were studied as involved in all sorts of forest proceedings (p. 74); manorial court rolls combed for reference to forest activities (213 ff). In the former case it was found that official perambulations proved to be very inadequate as sources for the investigations of forest activities; and, in the latter, it became clear that manorial courts handled much the same material as royal courts concerning forests but apparently without reference to the latter, and with the revelation of an extraordinary amount of individualistic activity on the forest frontier (220-221). For the East Midlands, the exhaustive work of Professor A. C. Chibnall on the Hundred of Newport Pagnell will illustrate, *inter alia*, the local features of settlement and assarting. The completely new approach required for study of forest society

This chapter is largely concerned with the data for one county, namely the assarting records to be found in the Forest Proceedings for the Royal Forest of Northamptonshire, records now housed in the Public Record Office, Chancery Lane. Appendices V to VII present the lesser data for assarts in counties bordering upon Northamptonshire. From the beginning of this century students of the forest have begun with G. J. Turner's edition *Select Pleas of the Forest*,[6] and Turner's description of the duties imposed upon those inquisitors called Regarders who reported or made a regard on assarts, purprestures and waste may still be considered as the best point of departure. The administrative routine identified, Turner's interest did not proceed to the historical fact of assarting, and it is important to notice that he did not edit any lists of assarts, and furthermore he rather misleadingly failed to indicate that lists of assarts had been omitted from his edited texts.[7]

In actual fact there are 34 extant reports from the Regarders for Northants forests over the thirteenth and early fourteenth century. At the same time, it would be difficult to discover a 'typical' report in this collection in the sense that Turner's introductory text is given as typical,[8] in so far as the Regarders were asked for varying degrees and sorts of information over this period — unlicensed assarts, old assarts, old assarts sown, old assarts sown since the last Regard, and by the fourteenth century, waste rented in the same fashion as assarts.[9] It follows, as might be expected, that there was considerable duplication of entries. And, in addition, over the whole of our period there are only about a score of the more full records of assarts.

What is most valuable for the historian, however, is not the number and variety of records but the survival of key lists of old assarts (*vetera assarta*). The *vetera assarta*, as Turner pointed out, indicate those assarts prior to the last Regard. The extant *vetera assarta* reports for Northamptonshire forests cluster about four

is well illustrated by Jean Birrell, "Peasant Craftsmen in the Medieval Forest", *Agricultural History Review*, 17 (1969), 91-107.

6 Selden Society, London, 1901.

7 E.g. the very first document edited, pp. 1-6, is followed by a list of assarts in the manuscript, though Turner makes no mention of this.

8 *Ibid.*, p. LXXVII. G. J. Turner was, of course, aware that forest legislation had evolved (cf. p. LXXV), but his concern was with the fully developed administration from the time of Henry III.

9 Cf. notes to table for further detail.

periods — the early thirteenth century, the mid-thirteenth century, towards the close of the thirteenth century, and late in the second quarter of the fourteenth century. Each group reports on the old assarts for approximately the previous two decades (or previous generation); and yet the old assarts from earlier than this generation are not included. We have therefore, a rather remarkably thorough accumulative picture of new assarting in the royal forests over the whole of this period as reported by the Regarders.

In the Appendices (I-IV) this information has been tabulated according to forest, and village in the forest. For brevity these data may be synopsized as follows:

TABLE I

FOUR GENERATIONS OF ASSARTS IN NORTHAMPTONSHIRE

	1st Gen.	2nd Gen.	3rd Gen.	4th Gen.	Acreage totals
Salcey Forest					
Villages & hamlets	18	8	3	?	
Assart units	33	22	3	34	
Assart acreage	284	91	12	558 :	945
Whittlewood					
Villages & hamlets	21	19	16	?	
Assart units	72	74	19	24	
Assart acreage	578	280	97	575 :	1530
Rockingham Forest					
Villages & hamlets	48	49	24	?	
Assart units	99	99	69	88	
Assart acreage	1286	797	812	1261 :	4156

In view of the vast acreage of the many villages involved the total acreage here is not impressive. But a search for absolute totals is undoubtedly illusory since assarts were a deliberately disappearing rather than a cumulative category of crown lands. That is to say, the great majority of assarting was permitted by grant of royal charter and the grantee was thereby excluded from the jurisdiction of the Regarders. Early in the thirteenth century this grant was frequently *post factum* so that the Regarders often did their work before the fact of licence was noted. In this way there comes to our attention the large blocks of land that did not come under the regular purview of the Regarders for even one generation. Of special note may be the 80 acres held by Robert de Nevil at Courteenhall, the 60 acres at Roade by the Abbot of St. James, the 80 acres at Duston by William of Duston, Geoffrey son of Peter's 60 acres at Abthorpe and 27 acres at Towcester, the 100 acres of the Hospitallers in a park area of Salcey, the 100 acres of the Abbot of Beck at Weedon Beck, the 500 acres by the monks of Pipewell at Rushton. Occasionally, the Regarders were still recording at the mid-century blocks of land asserted by grant of charter. Such were the 21 and 69 acre assart lots in Duddington held by John le Breton, the 26 acres in Stoke Doyle held by Robert de Ros, and units of 41, 17, 15 and 101/2 acres held by various religious houses. But from this time the Forest Proceedings begin to enroll various charters of grant to assart. Such for example is that of 1272, listing nine charters, though in only two cases are specific assart areas given.[10] While it may be too strong to suggest that such charters gave a *carte blanche* to assart, the general tenor of the charters indicates that a more total picture of land assarted must be gained through estate histories.[11]

Assart data from the Forest Proceedings, on the other hand, would seem to be better employed to indicate the chronology, the geographical location, and something of the scope and style of assarting. Some of these possibilities are sketched out in the next few pages.

To turn to chronology and geography in quite general terms, the small forest of Salcey represents most simply the various elements involved: first, the considerable perimeter of activity in the early thirteenth century (Courteenhall, Horton), secondly, the tendency towards many small assart units in some areas, especially towards the perimeter, and thirdly, evidence for some assart activity in all parts of the forest from the earliest thirteenth century although the units were larger and fewer towards the heart of the forest. After a flurry of activity at Horton over the 1240's and '50's the small nibbling had come to an end in Salcey forest. There was practically no assart activity reported in the time of Edward I. In the second quarter of the fourteenth century the old heart of the forest was farmed out in substantial units to various lords and their villages.

The Whittlewood Regard for the beginning of the thirteenth century was remarkably distant from the modern forest. Assarts

10 E. 32/72.

11 For Northants, the considerable possibilities of such histories is well illustrated by Chapter 4 of Dr Edmund King, *Peterborough Abbey, 1086-1310*, Cambridge, 1973.

were noted beyond the furthest mediaeval perambulations as far as Weedon Beck, many on the perimeter of the perambulation — at Towcester, Abthorpe, Burcote in one direction, and Cosgrove in another. These more distant assarts tend to appear in the records as larger blocks of land, perhaps, as already noted, because they were taken out of the Regarders' purview at this time by licence to various lords. Within what was to remain for sometime the forest of Whittlewood, yet beyond the modern core, there was as with Salcey evidence for much small unit activity over the whole first half of the thirteenth century. Grafton, Alderton, Norton and Westpery are particularly interesting in this respect.

Rockingham forest differed from the other forests of Northamptonshire in so far as, if an exception be made for the soke of Peterborough taken out of the forest from the time of John, the perimeter of this forest remained fairly stable throughout the thirteenth century. One could assume, therefore, that the administration of assarts became a more normal part of manorial life, and this may be the explanation for the fact that the assart units in most villages tended to be larger and to be held directly accountable to the king by the lord. Further, the strong influence of lordship in Rockingham is reflected in the earlier farming of waste than in other forests, fifteen units of waste being farmed before the end of the reign of Edward I. Still, a more detailed picture of the local scene is occasionally revealed. For instance, an outburst of small assarting appeared at Benefield and Rushton in the late thirteenth century.

The Regarders also left information about the tenure of assarts. It may be hazardous to distinguish a predominant social influence in Northamptonshire assarting before the fourteenth century. In what is the first document of our series[12] fines paid for assarting without licence in the royal forest are nearly all listed after the names of leading tenants-in-chief or mesne tenants. The considerable capital requirements for these fines may explain this in part. Furthermore, throughout the century for most assarts we are dealing with well established open-field villages, and the assart is described as *in campis* of such and such village. Inevitably, therefore, to the outside world initiative seems to lie with the lord. Even in villages where wood was held in severalty, as with Horton, assarts are said to be made by the

12 E 32/62 — 9 John.

owner 'of his own wood.' The good sequence of records for the second generation shows a tendency for assarts in Salcey and Whittlewood to move rather quickly into other hands from the one who was accounted for the actual assarting. Competition was apparently very keen for the last of this arable in these regions, and lay lords (like the king) were willing to make a quick profit from the land market. By contrast, however, in Rockingham Forest it was usual for the person identified as the orginal assarter to continue to hold the assart. A totally different picture appears in the fourteenth century with a decided pattern of engrossing in all forests.

But there is an 'underside' to the picture, and this occasionally peeps through even the formality of the records. Our first evidence for actual tenure, that above-mentioned document of 9 John, shows for the soke of Peterborough rather widely spread holdings among what would appear to be local people as well as the abbot, his obedientiaries, and his other associates. A glimpse at one type of local assart tenure is given by the two acres of assart at Gretton cleared and held there at the mid-century by Simon the Reeve, Hugh the Reeve, Walter the son of Norman, and Claricia de Gretton. And throughout the century one can occasionally see the small man, the virtual squatter, on the royal fee. For example, of the 16 units reported by the Regarders for Silverstone (Whittlewood) in the mid-thirteenth century, 8 are quarter-rod units upon which a house has been built and no corn sown. More often, however, it is the whole vill that has cleared and holds the assart: the vill of Thorpe holding 1/2 acre in 1209; the vill of Duddington holding assarts of 11 and 81/2 acres around the same time, as well as the vill of Nassington (2 acres), of King's Cliffe (57 and 4 acres), the 'men of Glapthorn' (1/2, 11/2, and 1/2 acre units); 'men of the abbey of Crowland' 14 acres at Glapthorn; vill of Corby (3 acres), of Burcote (1 rod), of Silverstone (10 and 2 acres). From the mid-thirteenth century no more vills are reported as holdings assarts in Salcey or Whittlewood. In Rockingham Forest the villagers held assart at Duddington (151/2 acres), King's Cliffe (5 acres) and Apethorpe (20 acres) at the mid-century. And in the third generation Duddington held 12 acres, Brigstock 30 acres, and Geddington 5 acres.

The historian's virtual ignorance of the techniques of assarting opens the door to many hypotheses. Was an assart made by a relatively poor man encroaching on easily cultivable waste and scratching up portions of a rod for sowing? Or, as has been suggested, was the capital and labour requirement for assarting such as to require mobilization of the resources of the whole village to clear even a few acres a year? Was assarting an individualistic imposition by lord or other on a communal woodland economy? Or, was assarting the traditional mode of expansion — the frontier response to population pressure in particular — for the whole village? The Northamptonshire evidence suggests support for each hypothesis at different places and times.

The assart texts contain considerable information about cropping, and from this a rather clear picture emerges. While Turner remarked that "the record seldom states the nature of the corn sown in the winter,"[13] and his general text from the articles of the charter of the forest refers to vague winter and spring sowing (*hibernagium* and *tramesium*), in all but two documents the Regarders of Northants give the type of corn sown. For the first generation of the thirteenth century the report on crops was for that year only, rather than all the sowings since the last Regard, and usually there is no reference to fallow.

In every instance at this time wheat or oats are reported: 13 of 33 sown units in Salcey forest, and 24 of 73 in Whittlewood, were sown partly in wheat and partly in oats, the proportion of each usually being one-half, but beyond this no discernible pattern may be found. These divided sowings were to be found in quite small units of one acre as well as large blocks of 80 or 100 acres. Is it to be assumed, therefore, that parts of such assarts lay in different open fields? Unfortunately our records do not help in this, at least in so far as my reading of them goes. One could as easily deduce that the two crop course was introduced within one assart unit in order to claim as quickly as possible the advantages of the inherent variety. For Rockingham (except in the soke of Peterborough), the ratio of oats to wheat sown tends to be much higher at this period, that is to say, where one crop is reported in some 2 of 3 instances this tends to be oats. Also, a much smaller proportion of the assarts in Rockingham are sown simultaneously in two types of corn, and again where there is divided sowing at Rockingham much the greater part (frequently as much as 2/3) is in oats.

Since the Regards for the second generation can be established in a clear chronological series, more information is available for cropping in the 1240's and '50's. Where there are specific

13 *Op. cit.*, p. LXXVIII.

references to first sowings on new assarts, in every instance these are in oats (Grafton and Weekley in Whittlewood; in Rockingham, Rushton, Gretton, Little Weldon, Faxton, Great Oakley, Deenethorpe; Horton in Salcey). This also remains true for many new assarts at Salcey and Whittlewood in the third generation (Appendix III, below).

In only one of the mid-century samples, that of Rushton, the first sowing of oats was followed by a fallowing, while in all other instances a sowing of wheat followed that of the first oats. Apparently a Regard had not taken place for sometime for Salcey and Whittlewood, so the first Regard of this second generation (1250) refers to the number of crops sown in particular fields since these had been asserted. Unfortunately, in only two instances are the number of years specified along with the crops sown. These are for two parcels in Grafton (Whittlewood) where the asserting was done 20 years before and 6 crops of oats and 6 of wheat had been taken since. In all other instances only the number of crops are given. For Salcey Forest, these are usually 2 or 3 only, that is on the assumption of a similiar rotation the clearings had been made in the mid 1240's. For Whittlewood many new fields had been cropped 6 or 8 times, suggesting assarting in the 1230's. Rockingham Forest croppings were uniformly 2 or 3, and our extant information about this forest was therefore, very likely preceded by a Regard that has been lost.

For the period of the various Regards in the 1250's the series is sufficient to give a complete picture of the crop rotation over several years. That is, there is a Regard for May, 1255 giving the crops sown at that time and those sown since the last Regard. We also have this last Regard, May, 1253, for the three forests, and a third Regard for 1250, all of these giving the same kind of information.[14]

Over the 1250's assarts sown in several parts were also to be found: 6 of 22 assarts at Salcey, 10 of 70 at Whittlewood, 15 of 98 in Rockingham Forest. More precisely, these entries usually refer to various 'parts' sown, in some cases the acreage is given rather than first, second or third part, and in one instance (Rockingham, no. 93-5) an assart is identified as 181/2 acres in three places.

This good run of information for sowings in the 1250's makes it clear that the wheat —oats— fallow course sequence was

14 Cf. Appendix II below.

followed in all the forests. The divided assarts just followed differing stages of the same sequence. By the third generation the rotation was considered to be automatic that is to say the specific sowings were not repeated for each assart.

Quite exceptional is the sowing of barley upon one-half of a small assart (3 acres, 31/2 rods) at Grafton in 1250, and at Plumpton in 1253, as neither sowing was repeated there or elsewhere. With the fourteenth century peas appear on the assarts of Rockingham Forest along with a crop of peas and oats mixed and of dredge. There was a gradual but not very rapid increase of mixed crops as this latter century progressed: peas and oats, oats and barley mixed, wheat and peas, barley and oats.

Very rarely was a piece of assart left uncultivated (*frisc'*) for some time in the earlier thirteenth century.[15] The number of such uncultivated units first becomes noticeable in Rockingham in 14 Edward I. Into the fourteenth century the category increases further, with some assart units apparently sown infrequently, some valued only for *subbosc'* and with many increasingly employed for pasture.

There is some useful information in the Forest Proceedings towards the economics of assarting. Nothing corresponding to an entry fine appears as an item of the regular Regard report. But our records do begin with a score of fines for assarts made without licence in 9 John. Unfortunately these do not give the size of the holdings, except in the one instance of one-half mark for 21/2 acres. By cross reference with other records of the period the size of some of the other properties sown in this list may be tentatively identified to give the following information: 4 sown acres at Grafton paid 20 s., 2 acres, 3 rods sown at Yardley paid 5 shillings, 1 acre, 1 rod sown at Piddington paid 12 d. The ten shilling fine paid by John de Wanville for 2 acres of assart sown at Grafton may be of the same order. In any case, neither from the fines paid by dominant tenants-in-chief for assarting without licence, nor from these identifiable small fines, does the amount seem to be excessive in terms of years of purchase.

This is particularly true in view of the 'value' of crops on various assarts as assessed in another document from the 10th year of King John.[16] The values are perhaps more interesting as indicating variety in soil rather than as averages.

15 In the good series of entries for Rockingham Forest for the mid century, Appendix II below, only numbers 9 and 50 indicate uncultivated assarts.

16 E 32/248.

TABLE II

VALUES OF SOME SOWN ASSARTS
(1208-1209)

PLACE[17]	*CROP ACREAGE*	*CROP VALUE*
Helmdon	6¹/2 a. oats	7s. 6d.
Astwell	1 a. 1r. wheat	3s.
Eastwell	3¹/2r. oats	3s.
Abthorpe	36¹/2 a. oats	50s.
Towcester	4 a. wheat, 2 a. oats	46s. 8d.
Silverstone	1 a. wheat	4s.
Whittlebury	2 a. oats, 1 a. part of rod wheat	7s.
Whittlebury	2 a. wheat, 6¹/2 a. oats	18s.
Pery	2 a. 1r. wheat	5s.
Pery	5 a. 1r. oats	2s.
Anderman	5 a. 1r. oats	10s. 6d.
Grafton	4 a. wheat	13s. 4d.
Grafton	1¹/2 a. wheat, 1¹/2 a. oats	5s. 6d.
Yardley	2 a. 3 r. oats	5s. 6d.
Piddington	4 a. wheat, 3 a. oats	22s. 4d.
Piddington	2 a. oats, 1 a. 3 r. wheat	10s. 6d.
Piddington	1 a. oats, 1 r. wheat	5s 1d.
Piddington	1 a. wheat	3s. 6d.
Weton (Wootton?)	6 a. wheat, 3¹/2 a. ¹/2r. oats	19s. 4d.
Hartwell	13¹/2 a. barley & oats, 1 a. 1 r. wheat	41s.
Roade	3 r. wheat, 1 r. oats	3s.
Stokes	3 r. oats	2s.
Stokes	1 a. wheat	3s. 6d.
Weedon (Beck)	3 a. oats	5s.

G. J. Turner pointed out that a regular payment had to be made to the king of a shilling per crop of winter corn, and sixpence per crop of spring corn.[18] Certainly in the Northants forests the shilling was paid for an acre of wheat and sixpence for an acre of oats with monotonous regularity from the beginning of the thirteenth century into the fourteenth century. Such fines were not paid when the land lay fallow. In view of the actual land values in the above table, this fine would not seem to have been a heavy burden. Cases of the royal agents taking land into their hands because it had been left idle are very rare. From the economics of land values and fines it is easy to see why assarting moved on apace and the sowing of wheat was as regular as that of oats in many places. At the same time, we do not know what the cost of assarting might have been, and whether the low fines allowed for that cost. The fact that the one assarting could not

17 In all the tables throughout this volume, where identification of a place has not been possible an effort is made to suggest the proper identity, or at least to leave sufficient manuscript spelling to assist others in doing so.

18 *Op. cit.*, p. LXXVIII.

pay initial costs by the sale of trees seems to be implied in the separate accounting of these in our records for the late thirteenth and early fourteenth century.

During the fourth generation a different sort of land valuation emerges with the straightforward leasing of the waste. At Salcey and Whittlewood there is some variation in the entry fines and yearly rent values, though the entry fine is usually 12d per acre and the rent 4d per acre. The first rentals at Rockingham are much more varied, the entry fine being as high as 18d per acre and as low as 4d, the annual rent varying from 6d to 2d. Undoubtedly this suggests much for the variety of soil. The last of the waste in Rockingham was much more uniform in value, usually going for 12d as fine and 4d as rent.

APPENDIX I

ASSARTING OF THE ROYAL FORESTS OF NORTHAMPTONSHIRE IN THE EARLY THIRTEENTH CENTURY

Introductory Notes:

1. It is useful to arrange as a first group in this series of records the list of personal fines for assarting *sine licentia*. Public Record Office E 32/62 (1209), membrane 2, appears to be the first record of this type. Another copy of the same document is to be found in E 32/249, membrane 15. While something of an overall indication of the rate of increase of assarts, this type of document — like the Pipe Roll entries — is of little value standing alone since the place of the assart is not given. Places are indicated in this record only for the Nassington liberty of Peterborough (membrane 3), and are exceptionally useful for the assarting situation in that region at the time this abbey zone was exempted from the forest laws (cf. Edmund King, *op. cit.*, Chapter 4).

2. Several other documents from this period may be gathered in a second group in so far as these documents concern themselves with older assarts reviewed to see if they are warranted (if not, fines were paid) and to assess the value of crops being grown. E 32/248 (1209) is the most complete of this group. (See Table II above, for some of the entries from this manuscript). (E 32/249, membrane 17, is a copy of the first membrane of E 32/248). E 32/249, membrane 12, is another list of old assarts for this year, but not useful since acreage and village location were not given. Furthermore, this latter document differs in personal names from the previous records in this group. Very likely, E 32/249, membrane 12, is entirely a report of fines for waste rather than assarts since one entry so specifies and the fines for other entries are the much smaller nominal fines usually expected for waste rather than those substantial fines for old assarts of this year.

3. For Salcey and Whittlewood forests, the most useful group for this first Generation are a complementary set of documents, E 32/249, membranes 6 and 13. The latter gives fines for crops of that year, though the date is not given; the former does not give fines, but includes much more detail about names, new assarts, and the splitting up of sowing on assarts. For this reason, membrane 6 is employed for tabulation whenever it clearly includes membrane 13. The existence of many of the assarts from 1209 (E 32/248) in membrane 6 and 13 suggests that these membranes come from late John or early Henry III.

While membrane 6 does not include Rockingham Forest, there is a detailed Regard from 10 John for Rockingham in E 32/249, membrane 11. Unfortunately portions of membrane 11 are faded away, but enough remains to form a useful complementary table with (the later) E 32/249, membrane 13.

4. In all the above documents, crop reports appear to be for the one year only. In short, the Regard system did not seem to report for a period of years so that very little can be done on rotation for this early period. Above all, the usual failure to report assarts in fallow could mean that totals for assarts sown at the time might indicate fully one-third or even one-half (assuming a three-course system) of assart acreage was not indicated.

5. The sequence of place names in the following table is as taken from the manuscripts. Since for the majority of villages identification has been readily established through the volumes of the Place-Name Society, it has been thought more convenient to render village names in modern spelling in these tables. Most of the place names not to be found on the modern Ordnance Map can be traced in the fine series of maps available in the volume of P. A. J. Pettit (*The Royal Forests of Northamptonshire — A study in their Economy, 1558-1714*, Northamptonshire Record Society, XXIII, 1968).

SALCEY FOREST

PLACE	*ASSART ACREAGE*	*CROP SOWN*
Courteenhall	80 a.	o.
	1 r.	w.
	1½ a.	o.
	1 r.	o.
	1½ a.	o.
	1 r.	o.
Hartwell	1 a.	w.
	3 a.	w.
	14 a.	o.
	4 a.	o.
Ashton	10 a. 1 r.	7 a. w.
		3 a. 1 r. o.
Harwell (Hartwell?)	1 a.	w.
Roade	1 a.	w.
	½ a.	w.
	60 a.	30 a. w.
		30 a. o.
Blisworth	29 a.	17 a. w.
		12 a. o.
Wulfey (? Wolfage: Brixworth)	17 a.	8 a. w.
		9 a. o.
Shutlanger	5 a.	w.
Shaw: Stoke Bruerne	6 a.	4 a. w.
		2 a. o.
Hulcote: Easton Neston	15 a.	7 a. w.
		8 a. o.
	15 a.	8 a. o.
		7 a. o.
Salcey	8 a.	4 a. w.
		4 a. o.
Horton	½a.	w.

SALCEY FOREST cont'd

Piddington	2 a.	1 a. w.
		1 a. o.
	1½ a.	1 a. w.
		½ a. o.
	1 a.	½ a. w.
		½ a. o.
	½ a.	1 r. w.
		1 r. o.
	1 a.	o.
Wootton	1 a.	o.
Stoke (Bruerne?)	1 r.	o.
Rothersthorpe	1 r.	o.
Stoke Park Ho: Stoke Bruerne	2½ a.	1½ a. w.
		1 a. o.
Preston (Deanery)	1 r.	o.

WHITTLEWOOD E32/249m6.

PLACE	*ASSART ACREAGE*	*CROP SOWN*
Harpole	9 a.	5 a. w.
		4 a. o.
Duston	80 a.	30 a. w.
		50 a.o.
	8 a.	3 a. w.
		5 a. o.
Weedon Beck	2 a.	w.
	100 a.	10 a. o.
Stowe Nine Churches	3 a.	1½ a. w.
		1½ a. o.
Blakesley	½ a.	w.
Astwell	9 a.	o.
	1½ a.	w.
Abthorpe	60 a.	25 a. w.
		35 a. o.
Paulerspury	3 a. 2 r.	2 a. 1 r. w.
		1 a. 1 r. o.
	2 a.	w.
	3 a.	2 a. o.
		1 a. w.
	1 a.	o.
	3 a.	1 a. w.
		2 a. o.
	3 a.	o.
	1 r.	w.
	100 a.	50 a. w.
		50 a. o.
	3 r.	1 r. w.
		2 r. o.
	22 a.	o.
	3 a.	o.
	1 a.	o.
	3 a.	o.

WHITTLEWOOD cont'd

PLACE	*ASSART ACREAGE*	*CROP SOWN*
Cosgrove	4 a.	o.
	3 a.	w.
	1 a.	o.
	½ a.	o.
Wicken	10 a.	5 a. w.
		5 a. o.
	1½ a.	w.
Whittlebury	12 a.	6 a. w.
		6 a. o.
	2 a.	w.
	3 a.	o.
	1½ a.	1 a. w.
		½ a. o.
	1 r.	o.
	1 r.	o.
	1 r.	o.
Towcester	27 a.	13 a. w.
		14 a. o.
Wood Burcote: Towcester	5½ a.	3 a. w.
		2½ a. o.
	1 r.	w.
	1 a.	½ a. w.
		½ a. o.
	3 a.	2 a. w.
		1 a. o.
	2½ a.	1 a. w.
		1½ a. o.
	32 a.	12 a. o.
		19 a. o.
	3 a.	1 a. w.
		2 a. o.
	½ a.	o
Plumpton End: Paulerspury	11 a.	6 a. w.
		5 a. o.
Alderton	½ a.	o.
Grafton Regis	2½ a.	w.
	4 a.	w.
	1 a.	o.
Furtho	2 a.	1 a. w.
		1 a. o.
Helmdon	1 a.	
Silverstone	1 a.	o.
	1 a.	½ a. w.
		½ a. o.
	1 r.	o.
	½ a.	o.
	½ a.	o.
	½ r.	o.
	½ a.	o.
	3 a.	w.
	½ a.	w.
	1 r.	o.
	1 r.	o.
	1 r.	o.

WHITTLELEWOOD cont'd

PLACE	*ASSART ACREAGE*	*CROP SOWN*
Silverstone	1 r.	w.
	1 r.	o.
	1/2 a.	w.
	1 r.	w.
	10 a.	6 a. w.
		4 a. o.
	2 a.	o.
Blisworth	1 1/2 a.	w.
Blakesley (Hachesull Park)	100 a.	w.
Horton	1 r.	?

ROCKINGHAM FOREST ASSARTS

	E32/249 m 11.	E32/249 m 13.
PLACE	*t. John*	
Rothwell	1 r.	—
Desborough	6 a.	6 a.
Braybrooke	3 a.	1 1/2 a.
East Carlton	5 a.	5 a. ?
	6 a.	6 a.
	6 a.	6 a.
Rushton	5 a.	5 a. (+?)
	3 a.	3 a.
	2 a.	2 a.
	2 a.	2 a.
	1/2 a.	1 1/2 a.
(Rushton?)	500 a.	—
Colershawe	14 a.	—
Rohawe & Essawe (Wilbarston)	15 a.	—
Oakley	5 1/2 a.	5 1/2 a. ?
	4 a.	—
Oakley, Little	1 r.	—
Oakley, Great	3 a.	—
Stanion	13 1/2 a.	13 1/2 a.
	1 a.	1 a.
	3 a.	3 a.
	—	1/2 a.
Corby	3 a.	3 a.
	1 r.	—
Geddington	1/2 a.	—
	1/2 a.	1/2 a.
	1/2 a.	1/2 a.
	3 a.	—
Newton	1 1/2 a.	1 1/2 a.
	1/2 a.	—
Slipton	5 r.	4 a.
?	1/2 a.	—
Brigstock	2 1/2 a. 5 r.	2 1/2 a.
	10 a.	7 a.
	5 a.	5 a.
Sudborough	1 r.	1 r.
Lowick	3 r.	3 r.
	3 r.	3 r.

ROCKINGHAM FOREST cont'd

PLACE	E32/249 m 11 *t. John*	E32/240 m 13
Lowick	3 a. 1 r.	2 a.
	—	1 a.
	—	1 r.
Wadenhoe	29½ a.	34 a.
Pilton	12 a.	12 a.
Stoke Doyle	9½ a.	9½ a.
	7½ a.	2 a.
Old & New Lyveden:		3 a.
Aldwinkle	12 a.	12 a.
	7 a.	7 a.
Benefield	44 a.	1 a.
	—	1 a.
	—	1 a.
	—	1 a.
	—	½ a.
	—	16 a.
Southwick	1½ a.	3½ a.
	—	3 r.
	1½ a.	3 a.
	—	4 a.
	1 a.	1 a.
	½ a.	½ a.
	4½ a. 3 r.	4½ a.
	2 a.	—
Glapthorn	2 a.	1 a.
	1 a.	1 a.
	—	1 r.
	½ a.	—
	½ a.	½ a.
	½ a.	1½ a.
	1 a.	1 a.
	14 a.	14 a.
	4½ a.	½ a.
		3 a.
	5½ a.	4 a.
	—	3 a.
Cotterstock	—	4 a.
Duddington	8½ a.	8½ a.
	16 a.	11 a.
	4 a.	—
	1 a.	—
Nassington	1 r.	2 a.
	1 a.	2 a.
	1½ a.	4 a.
	—	3 r.
	—	3 r.
Yarwell	1 a.	1 a.
King's Cliffe	60 a.	61 a.

ROCKINGHAM FOREST cont'd

PLACE	E32/249 m 11	E32/249 m 13
Sub Piri (Southwick)	15 a.	5 a.
		1½ a.
		2½ a.
Hale (Apethorpe)	3 a.	3 a.
Wakerley	23 a.	3 a.
		30 a.
		8 a.
Laxton	17 a.	3 a.
	1 a.	1 a.
	—	30 a.
Easton-on-the-Hill	(10) a.	—
Blatherwycke	4 a. +	—
?	7½ a.	—
?	15 a.	—
?	6½ a.	—
?	30 a.	—
?	?	—
?	?	—
Burgh property-		
Hundred (Suhawe)	25 a.	—
(Ufford: Southey Wood)	3 a.	4 a.(Undele)
	80 a.	—
Deene	45 a.	52 a.
Bulwick	8 a.	30 a.
		2½ a.
Henwick: Bulwick	2 a.	10 a.
Harringworth	26 a.	26 a.
Kirby Hall: Gretton	4½ a.	2½ a.
	6 a.	3½ a.
Gretton	2 a.	—
Cotton: Gretton	1 a.	6 a.
Weldon, Great and Little	6 a.	6 a.
	1 a.	—
	3 r.	1 r.
	—	1 r.
	—	1 r.
	—	1 r.
Deenethorpe	15 a.	—
Rockingham	30 a.	—
	9 a.	—
Rising Bridge: Geddington	—	½ a.
Helpston	—	½ a.
	—	1 a.
Woodcroft Castle: Etton	—	½ a.
	—	2 a.
	—	2 a.
	—	2 a.

ROCKINGHAM FOREST cont'd

PLACE	E32/249 m 11	E32/249 m 13
Halwton (Alwalton?)	—	1 a.
Walton	—	2½ a.
	—	1 a.
Falshelm	—	1½ a.
Paston	—	3 a.
	—	1 r.
	—	1½ a.
	—	5½ a.
	—	½ a.
	—	2½ a.
	—	2 a.
Wychenmord (Wansford?)	—	1 a.
	—	5½ a.
Walton	—	[—]
	—	2½ a.
[Cotsm]	—	1 a.
	—	1 a.
	—	(6 a.)
Stodinton (Sutton?)	—	1 a.
	—	4 a.
Upton	—	4½ a.
	—	5 a.
	—	1 a.
	—	3 a.
West Wood: Thornhaugh	—	3 a.
	—	1 r.
Castor	—	1 a.
	—	1 r.
Southorpe	—	1½ a.

APPENDIX II

MID-THIRTEENTH-CENTURY ASSART DATA FOR NORTHAMPTONSHIRE FORESTS

Introductory Notes

1. The mid-thirteenth-century assarting picture for Salcey and Whittlewood forests is easily available in the three manuscripts E32/64 (34 H III), E32/66 (37 H III) and E32/69 (39 H III). The date of the last document is further specified as Pentecost, i.e. May 16th, 1255. Since, given the number of crops noted on May 16th, 1255, there cannot have been another Regard since that of 37 H III and both spring and winter crops are reported for the two years, E32/66 may be further specified as spring (May!), 1253. Unfortunately, the 1253 Regard notes crops sown for that year only, so it is not possible to indicate the rotation since 34 H III. For the following table the latter document is dated as 1250.

The records for assarting at Rockingham Forest in the mid-thirteenth century cover approximately the same years as that of the other Northants forests. The Public Record Office dating of the basic record, E32/67 as (36), 37 and 39 H III, might better be (34), 37 and 39 H III from the cropping information indicated by the 37 H III entries. The (34) H III entries only break in half-way through the Regarder's report (at 56 in the following list) but there is a fragment for May 3rd, 1250 as membrane 28 of E32/249, that supplies most of the missing information (1-47; unfortunately nearly one-half of these entries are faded away). A further manuscript, E32/68, reports numbers 57 to 77 for 1255 (E32/67) without adding any useful detail upon assarts, although from a few tenurial changes it is clear that E32/68 is not an exactly contemporaneous copy.

2 The method employed for tabulation of sowing can be most easily explained by an illustration. As the Regarders looked back to the sowing since the time of the previous regard, the student may begin with the last entry of the series. To take entry number 78 for Rockingham Forest as an example:

Vitalis Dengayne assartavit aput Neuton .xi. acras et dimidiam de feodo suo proprio. Unde Henricus filius eius qui tenet nihil recepit post ultimum regardum. Sed modo in bladum frumento. (E32/67, m. 6-39 H III [1255]).

Vitalis de engoyne assartavit aput Neuton .xi. acras et dimidiam de feodo suo proprio. Unde Henricus filius eius qui dictum assartum tenet recepit post ultimum regardum .j. vesturam frumenti et modo inbladatur avene (E32/67, m. 3-37 H III [1253]).

Vitalis de Engayne assartavit aput Neuton .xi. acras et dimidiam de feodo suo proprio. Unde Henricus filius eius qui dictum assartum tenet recepit inde postea .ii. vesturas frumenti et unam de avene et modo inbladatur avene. (E32/67, m. 1-35 H III [1250]).

Henry Engayne received no crop after the regard of 1253 since for the intervening year the assart lay fallow. Fallow (*warect'*) acres were only indicated for the current year (*modo*), but the rotation cycle of wheat-oats-fallow-wheat was so regular that fallowing seasons could be easily interpolated for the following table, at least back to 1250. This regular rotation seemed to pertain to assart subdivided into two or more fields, although as may be seen from the following first entry from Rockingham Forest, one must assume that the fields of the assart were reported in the same sequence by every regard:

Et jurati dicunt quod Adam de Pyrinton dominus de Faxton assartavit Fackel de feodo suo proprio et continet in se per estimationem .L xi. acras et pertinet ad manerium suum de Faxton. Unde recepit post ultimum regardum de .xx. acris et dimide .l. vesturam frumenti et modo in bladum avene. Et de .xx. acris et dimidie .l. vesturam avene et modo iacent warecte. Et .xx. acris in bladum frumento, et dictus Adam dictum assartum adhuc tenet. (E32/67, m. 6-39 H III [1255]).

Et jurati dicunt quod dominus Adam de Pyriton dominus de Faxton assartavit Fackel de feodo suo proprio et continet in se per estimationem .Lxi. acras et pertinet ad manerium suum de Faxton. Unde dictus Adam qui dictum assartum tenet recepit post ultimum regardum .ii. vesturas de .ii. partibus dicti assarti. Unde .i. de frumento et .i. de avene et modo inbladantur due partes frumento et avene et tertia pars iacet Warecta. (E32/67, m. 3-37 H III [1253]).

3. Undoubtedly a detailed study of the tenants would make possible a more precise first dating for the time of the actual assart. In general, since many of the tenants credited with the original assart were still holding in 1250, it may be deduced that most of the assarts in these Northants forests took place over the 1230's and 1240's. It is difficult to specify the dates of actual assarting for Rockingham since, as the 1250 column of the following table shows, the number of crops reported prior to the 1250 regard are so uniform that very likely another regard preceded that of 1250. For Salcey Forest the last regard (ultimam estimationem) is usually referred to, and this explains the fairly regular numbers of crops prior to 1250. For Whittlewood Forest, on the other hand, the total number of crops since assarting are specified, so that it would be possible (assuming a regular rotation) to reconstruct the dates for very active assarting in this forest over the 1230's and 1240's.

SALCEY FOREST CROPS

NAME	*ACREAGE*	*1250*	*1253*	*1255*
1. Burnewode (Horn Wood: Easton Maudit)? (Tiffield)	11½ a.	(?) 1 o. + 2 w. ?	w.	w. + o.
2. Burnewode (Horn Wood: Easton Maudit)? (Tiffield) (waste)	½ a.	nil	nil	f.
3. Easton Neston	3 a. 1 r.	(?) 1? o. + w. + f.	f.	nil + w.
4. Horton	1½ a. ½ r.	(2) 1 o. + 1 (w?). + ?	f.	o. + w.
5. Horton	1½ a. ½ r.	(3) 2 w. + 1 o.	o.	o. + w.
6. Horton	4 a.	(3) 2 w. + 1 o.	o.	o. + w.
7. Horton	2½ a.	(3) 1 o. + 2 w. + f.	o.	w. + o.
8. Horton	5 a. 1.9/10 r.	2 o. ( ); (10) 3 w. + 2 o.	1 part — f.	
		(3) 2 o. + 1 w. + f.	other part — f.	o. + (w).
9. Horton	5½ a. ½ r.	1 o;	one part — w.	o. + w.
		(5) 3 o. + 2 w;		
		(3) 1 o. + 2 w. + o.	other part — w.	o. + w.
10. Horton	14 a. 1 r.	(8) 4 o. + 4 w;	one part — o.	o. + w.
		(3) 1 o. + 2 w. + o.	other part — o.	
11. Horton	4½ a. ½ r.	(2) 1 o. + 1 w. + o.	o.	o. + w.
12. Horton	3 a. 1 r.	(2) 1 w. + 1 o. + w.	w.	w. + o. + f.
13. Horton	6 a. 1 r.	(1) 1 o; (2) w. + 1 o. + 1 o. + f.	o.	w. + o.
14. Horton	4 a. 1 r.	(3) 2 o. + 1 w. + ½ w.	½ in w. &	½: w. + o. + f.
		+ ½ o.	½ in o.	½: o. + w.
15. Cogenhoe	3 a. 1 r.	(3) 2 w. + 1 o. + o.	o.	w. + o.
16. Cogenhoe	3 a. ½ r.	(3) 2 o. + 1 w. + w.	w.	w. + o.
17. Piddington	1 a.	(3) 2 o. + 1 w. + f.	o.	w. + o.
18. Quinton	4½ a. ⅓ r.	(3) 2 o. + 1 w. + ½ w.	2 parts in o.	½: w. + o. + f.
		+ ½ f.	3 parts in w.	½: w. + o.
19. Quinton	6 a. 1½ r.	(3) 2 w. + 1 o. (½ w.	½ w.	½ w. + f.
		(½ o.	½ o.	½ a. + w.
20. Ashton	3 a. ½ r.	(3) 2 w. + 1 o. + o.	o.	o. + w.
21. Ashton	3 a. 1.8/10 r.	(3) 2 w. + 1 o. + o.	o.	a. + w.
22. Ashton	2½ a. 1 r.	(3) 2 o. + 1 w. + o.	o.	

WHITTLEWOOD FOREST CROPS

NAME	*ACREAGE*	*1250*	*1253*	*1255*
1. Grafton	$3\frac{1}{2}$ a. 1 r.	(20 yrs, 12 crops) 6 o. + 6 w.	w.	o.
2. Grafton	$1\frac{1}{2}$ a. $\frac{1}{3}$ r.	(4) 2 o. + 2 w.	w.	no data
3. Grafton	1. $\frac{1}{3}$ r.	(4) 2 o. + 2 w.	w.	1 w. + 1 o. + f.
4. Grafton	2 a. $\frac{1}{2}$ r. $\frac{5}{6}$ r.	(4) 2 o. + 2 w.	w.	w + o.
5. Grafton	3 a. $3\frac{1}{2}$ r.	(20 years, 12 crops) 6 o. + 6 w.	$\frac{1}{2}$ w.	f.
		($\frac{1}{2}$ w. $\frac{1}{2}$ barley?)	$\frac{1}{2}$ o.	
6. Yardley	$8\frac{1}{2}$ a.	(4) 2 w. + 2 o.	o.	w. + o.
7. Alderton	1 a. $1\frac{1}{2}$ r.	(4) 2 w. + 2 o.	o.	o.
8. Alderton	$\frac{1}{2}$ r. $\frac{4}{5}$ r.	(6) 3 o. + 3 w.	o.	o.
9. Alderton	$2\frac{1}{2}$ a.	(10) 5 w. + 5 o. + o.	o.	o.
10. Alderton	$2\frac{1}{2}$ r.	(10) 5 w. + 5 o. + o.	o.	w. + o.
11. Alderton	$\frac{4}{5}$ r.	(6) 3 o. + 3 w; (2) 1 o. + 1 w.	w.	no data
12. Plumpton End: Paulerspury	2 a. 3 r. $\frac{3}{4}$ r.	(8) 4 o. + 4 w. + o.	o.	
13. Plumpton End: Paulerspury	4 a.	(10) 5 w. + 5 o. + o.	barley	o.
14. ?	$10\frac{1}{2}$ a.	(9) 5 w. + 4 o. + o.	f.	w. + o.
15. Westpery: Paulerspury	3 r. $\frac{4}{5}$ r.	(7) 4 w. + 3 o. + o.	o.	o. + w.
16. Westpery: Paulerspury	1 a. $\frac{1}{2}$ r.	f.	f.	f.
17. Westpery: Paulerspury	$1\frac{1}{2}$ a.	(8) 4 o. + 4 w.	o.	o. + w.
18. Westpery: Paulerspury	10 a. $\frac{1}{2}$ r.	(6) 3 o. + 3 w.	o.	o. + w.
19. Westpery: Paulerspury	1 r. $\frac{3}{4}$ r.	f.	f.	nil
20. Westpery: Paulerspury	4 a.	(10) 5 o. + 5 w.	f.	o. + w.
21. Westpery	19 a.	(12) 6 o. + 6 w. + $\frac{1}{2}$ w.	$\frac{1}{2}$ w.	$\frac{1}{2}$: o + w.
		$\frac{1}{2}$ o.	$\frac{1}{2}$ o.	$\frac{1}{2}$: w. + o.
22. Westpery	9 a.	(12) 6 o. + 6 w. + o.	o.	o. + w.
23. Westpery	3 a.	10 o. + 9 w.	f.	o. + w
24. Green's Norton	1 a. 1 r. $\frac{2}{3}$ r.	(4) 2 w. + 2 o. + f.	f.	w. + o.
25. Green's Norton	2 a. $\frac{1}{2}$ r.	(5) 3 w. + 2 o. + o.	o.	o. + w.
26. Green's Norton	2 a. $\frac{1}{2}$ r.	(12) 6 w. + 6. o. + $\frac{1}{2}$ o.	f.	$\frac{1}{2}$: o. + (o?
		$\frac{1}{2}$ f.		$\frac{1}{2}$: w. + o.

WHITTLEWOOD FOREST cont'd

NAME	*ACREAGE*	*1250*	*1253*	*1255*
27. Green's Norton	1 1/2 r.	(5) 3 w. + 2 o. + o.	o.	o. + w.
28. Green's Norton	2 a. 1/2 r.	1 o. + 2 w. + o.	o.	o. + w.
29. Green's Norton	2 1/2 a. $\frac{10}{11}$ r.	(5) 2 w. + 3 o; w + o. + f.	f.	o. + w.
30. Green's Norton	1 a. 3 r. $\frac{10}{11}$ r.	(6) 3 w. + 3 o;	o.	o. + w.
		(5) 3 w. + 2 o. + o.		
31. Green's Norton	6 a. 2/3 r.	(7) 4 w. + 3 o. + 1/2 w.	1/2 w.	1/2: w. + o. + f.
		1/2 o.	1/2 o.	1/2: o. + w.
32. Green's Norton	9 a.	(12) 6 w. + 6 o. + 1/2 o.	1/2 o.	1/2: o. + w. + f.
		1/2 w.	1/2 f.	1/2: o. + w.
33. Green's Norton	8 a.	(7) 4 o. + 3 w. + 1/2 w.	1/2 w.	1/2: w. + o. + f.
		1/2 o.	1/2 o.	1/2: o. + w.
34. Hoggenhul (Blakesley?) (Bucknell Wood: Abthorpe)	purprestura	same	same	
35. (Blakesley?) (Bucknell Wood: Abthorpe)	3 a. 3/4 r.	(6) 3 w. + 3 o. ; + f.	f.	?
36. Astwell	4 a. 2/3 r.	(4) 2 w. + 2 o. + o.	o.	?
37. Litleley (Little Haw: Wilbarston?)	16 a.	(19) 10 o. + 9 w. + 1/2 o.	1/2 w.	
		1/2 w.	1/2 o.	
38. Bickenho (Syresham)	25 a. 2/3 r.	(12) 6 w. + 6 o. + o.	1/2 o.	
			1/2? (f?)	
39. Bickenho (Syresham)	3 a.	(8) 4 w. + 4 o. + f.	f.	
40. Silverstone	2 a. 1/2 r.	f.	f.	
41. Silverstone	1 a.	o.	o.	
42. Silverstone	1/2 r.	nil	nil	
43. Silverstone	4 parts of 1/2 r.	(4) f.	frisc'	
44. Silverstone	4 parts of 1 r.	nil	nil	
45. Silverstone	4 parts of 1/2 r.	nil	nil	

WHITTLEWOOD FOREST cont'd

NAME	*ACREAGE*	*1250*	*1253*	*1255*
46. Silverstone	2 parts of 1 r.	nil	nil	
47. Silverstone	4 parts of 1/2 r.	nil	nil	
48. Silverstone	1/2 r.	nil	nil	
49. Silverstone	4 th part of 1 r.	nil	nil	
50. Silverstone	4 parts of 1 r.	nil	nil	
51. Silverstone	5 a. 1 r.	8 w. + 8 o. + f.	f.	
52. Silverstone	2 a. 1/2 r.	8 w. + 8 o. + f.	f.	
53. Silverstone	10 a.	(14) 7 w. + 7 o. + o.	o.	
54. Silverstone	5 a.	(14) 7 w. + 7 o. + f.	f.	
55. Silverstone	purprestura of 1/2 r.	2 o. + w. + o.	o.	
56. fee of Linton	1 a.	o. + o.	o.	
57. Wicken	4 a.	(4) 2 o. + 2 w. + o.	o.	
58. Wicken	9 1/2 a. 5 parts 1 r.	(3) 2 o. + w. + f.	f.	
59. Wicken	6 a. 4 parts of 1 r.	(4) 2 w. + 2 o. + o.	o.	
60. Wicken	6 a. 1/2 r.	(5) 3 o. + 2 w. + o.	o.	
61. Wicken	8 a. 1/2 r.	(7) 4 o. + 3 w.	nil	
62. Barne?	8 1/2 a. 1/2 r.	(6) 3 o. + 3 w; (2) w. + o: 1/2 w.	o.	
63. Barne?	2 a. 1 r.	(2) w. + o; w. + o. 1/2 o.	o.	
64. Puxley: (Passenham)	4 parts of 1 r. (7 cottages)	nil	nil	
65. Puxley: (Passenham)	1 1/2 a. 2 parts of 1 r.	(12) 6 w. + 6 o.	o.	
66. Brgde (Passenham)	10 parts of 1 r.	(5) 3 o. + 2 w.		
67. Scrob Passenham	purprestura part of 1 r.	nil		
68. Ospery (East Perry?)	10 a. 1 r.			
	4 parts of 1 r.	(6) 3 w. + 3 o. + o.	o.	
69. Sweteleye (Weteley Wood: Syresham)	4 1/2 a.	(8) 4 w. + 4 o; w. + o.	o.	
70. Sweteleye (Weteley Wood: Syresham)	5 r.	o; o;	o.	

ROCKINGHAM FOREST CROPS

NAME	*ACREAGE*	*1250*	*1253*	*1255*
1. Faxton	61 a.	2 w + o. + o.	w. + o. + w.	20½ a. - w. + o.
		2 w. + o. + o.	w. + o. + o.	20½ a. - o. + f.
		f.	+ f.	20 a. - w.
2. Faxton	5½ a.	2 w. + o. + f.	w. + o. + f.	w. + o.
3. Thorpbelet	17 a.	2 o. + w. + w.	w. + o. + w.	w. + o.
		w.	w. + o. + o.	w. + o.
		f.	+ f.	f.
4. Newbottle	4½ a.	2 o. + w. + w.	o. + w.	o. + f.
5. Dingley	7½ a.	2 o. + w. + ½ w.	w. + o. + w.	w. + o.
		½ o.	w. + o. + o.	w. + o.
		½ o.	f.	f.
6. Brampton Ash	1 r.	2 w. + o. + o.	w. + o.	nil + w.
7. Brampton Ash	1 r.	2 w. + o. + o.	w. + o.	nil + w.
8. Brampton Ash	4 a.	w. + o. + o.	o. + w.	o. + f.
9. Brampton Ash	2½ r.	frisc'	frisc'	frisc'
10. Brampton Ash	1 a.	w. + o. + w.	o. + w.	o. + f.
11. Brampton Ash	2½ a.	2 w. + o. + o.	w. + o.	nil + w.
12. Brampton Ash	1½ a.	2 w. + o. + o.	w. + o.	nil + w.
13. Brampton Ash	9 a. 1 r.	2 w. + o. + o.	w. + o.	nil + w.
14. Brampton Ash	5 a.	2 w. + o. + o.	w. + o.	nil + w.
15. Desborough	9½ a. (10½)	2 w. + o. + o.	w. + o.	nil + w.
16. Rushton	11 a.	6 a: w. + 2 o. + f.	6 a: 2 w. + o. + f.	6 a: w. + o.
		5 a: 2 w. + o. + o.	5 a: w. + o.	5 a: nil + w.
17. Rushton	1 r.	2 w. + o. + o.	w. + o.	nil + w.
18. Burgwode (Cottingham?)	12 a.	w. + (2) o. + f.	w. + o. + f.	w. + o.
19. Wyberdel	26 a.	16 a: (2) w. + o. + w.	16 a: w. + o.	16 a: nil + w.
(Wilbarston)		10 a: f. + o.	10 a: w. + o. + f.	10 a: w. + o.
20. Cottingham	8½ a.	w. + 2 o. + f.	w. + o. + f.	w. + o.
21. Corby	3 a.	(2) o. + w. + f.	w. + o. + f.	w. + o.
22. Corby	1 r.	2 o. + w. + f.	w. + o. + f.	w. + o.

ROCKINGHAM FOREST cont'd

NAME	*ACREAGE*	*1250*	*1253*	*1255*
23. Little Weldon	1/2 a.	2 w. + o. + ?	w. + o.	nil + w.
24. Deene	8 1/2 a.	2 o. + w. + (f?)	w. + o. + f.	w. + o.
25. Deene	10 a.	2 o. + w. + f.	w. + o. + f.	w. + o.
26. Deenethorpe	4 1/2 a.	2 w. + o. + o.	w. + o.	nil + w.
27. Great Weldon	2 a.	w. + 2 o. + f.	w. + o. + f.	w. + o.
28. Great Oakley	15 a. 1 r.	? + ? + f.	w. + o. + f.	w. + o.
29. Newton	3 a. 1 r.	2 w. + ? + o.	w. + o. + f.	w. + o.
30. Weekley	20 a. 1 r.	? ? ?	w. + o.	nil + w.
31. Grafton Underwood	2 a.	w. + o. + w.	o. + w.	o. + f.
32. Lowick	8 a.	5 a: ? + ? + f. 3 a: w. + o. + o.	5 a: w. + o. + f. 3 a: w. + o.	5 a: w. + o. 3 a: nil + w.
33. Wadenhoe	4 a.	? ? ?	w. + o. + f.	w. + o.
34. Wadenhoe	3 a.	2 w. + ? + ?	w. + o.	nil + w.
35. Pilton?	5 a.	w. + o. + w.	w. + o.	nil + w.
36. Stoke Doyle	11 a.	w. + 2 o. + f.	w. + o.	nil + w.
37. Benefield	1 1/2 a.	in the king's hands?	?	?
38. Lyveden: Aldwinkle	7 a.	? + ? + o.	w. + o.	nil + w.
39. Sudborough	26 a.	2 o. + ? + ?	w. + o. + f.	w. + o.
40. Gretton	28 a.	? + ? + o.	w. + o.	nil + w.
41. East Carlton	3 a.	2 o. + w. + f.	w. + o. + f.	w. + o.
42. Cottingham	12 a.	? + w. + o.	w. + o.	nil + w.
43. Little Weldon	1/2 r.	? + ? + o.	w. + o.	nil + w.
44. Deene	3 a.	? ? ?	w. + o.	nil + w.
45. Great Weldon	20 a.	? ? ?	w. + o.	nil + w.
46. Stanion	2 a. 1/2 r.	? ? ?	o. + w.	o. + f.
47. Little Oakley	3 a.	? ? ?	w. + o. + f.	w. + o.
48. Great Oakley	1 r.	? ? ?	w. + o.	nil + w.
49. Newton	1 a.	? ? ?	w. + o. + f.	w. + o.
50. Aldwinkle: All Saints and St. Peter	1/2 a.	? ? ?	frisc'	frisc'

ROCKINGHAM FOREST cont'd

NAME	*ACREAGE*	*1250*	*1253*	*1255*
51. Stoke Doyle	3 a.	? ? ?	w. + o.	nil + w.
52. Churchfield Farm: Benefield	7 a.	? ? ?	w. + o. + f.	w. + o.
53. Benefield	9 a.	? ? ?	w. + o.	nil + w.
54. Sudborough	2 a.	? ? ?	w. + o. + f.	w. + o.
55. Gretton	2 a.	? ? ?	o. + w.	o. + w. + f.
56. Aldwinkle: All Saints and St. Peter	1½ r.	2 w. + o. + o.	w. + o.	nil + w.
56a. Suardshawe (Sewardsley: Easton Neston?)	30½ a.	w. + o. + f.	w. + o. + f.	w. + o.
57. Glapthorn	16½ a.	8 a: w. + o. + f.	w. + o.	nil + w.
		8½ a: o. + w. + (o?)		
58. Southwick	1 a.	(2) o. + w. + f.	w. + o. + f.	w. + o.
59. Duddington	15½ a.	(2) 2 o. + w. + f.	w. + o. + f.	w. + o.
60. Duddington	5½ a.	2 o. + w. + (⅓ f.	2 parts o. + w.	2 parts o. + f.
		(2 parts w.	3 rd part w. + o. + f.	3 rd part w. + o.
61. Duddington	21½ a.	9½ a: 2 o. + w. + f.	9½ a: w. + o. + f.	9½ a: w. + o.
		12 a: 2 w. + o. + o.	12 a.: w. + o.	12 a: (nil?) + w.
62. Duddington	69 a.	23 a: 2 o. + w. + f.	23 a: w. + o. + f.	23 a: w. + o.
		23 a: w. + o. + w.	23 a.: o. + w.	23 a: o. + f.
		23 a: 2 w. + o. + o.	23 a: w. + o.	23 a: nil + w.
63. Weston	1 a.	2 o. + w. + f.	w. + o. + f.	w. + o.
64. King's Cliffe	5 a.	w. + o. + w.	o. + w.	w. + o.
65. Bulwick	4 a.	2 o. + w. + f.	w. + o. + f.	w. + o.
66. Apethorpe	4½ a.	o. + w. + o.	w. + o.	nil + w.
67. Bulwick	19½ a.	10½ a: 2 o. + w. + f.	10½ a: w. + o. + f.	10½ a: w. + o.
		9 a: 2 w. + o. + o.	9 a: w. + o.	9 a: nil + w.
68. Bulwick	9½ a.	w. + o. + w.	o. + w.	o. + f.
69. Bulwick	15 a.	2 o. + w. + f.	w. + o. + f.	w. + o.
70. Blatherwycke	½ a.	w. + o. + w.	o. + w.	o. + f.

ROCKINGHAM FOREST cont'd

NAME	*ACREAGE*	*1250*	*1253*	*1255*
71. Hale: Apethorpe	$8\frac{1}{2}$ a.	w. + o. + w.	o. + w.	o. + f.
72. Sibberton: Thornhawe	$\frac{1}{2}$ a.	w. + o. + w.	o. + w.	o. + f.
73. Southwick	$5\frac{1}{2}$ a.	2 w. + o. + o.	w. + o.	nil + w.
74. Southwick	$1\frac{1}{2}$ a.	2 w. + o. + o.	w. + o.	nil + w.
75. Apethorpe	20 a.	2 w. + o. + o.	w. + o.	(nil + w)
76. Southwick	1 a.	2 w. + o. + o.	w. + o.	nil + w.
77. Hale: Apethorpe	$5\frac{1}{2}$ a.	2 w. + o. + o.	w. + o.	nil + w.
78. Woodnewton	$11\frac{1}{2}$ a.	2 w. + o. + o.	w. + o.	nil + w.
79. Laxton	$\frac{1}{2}$ a.	2 w. + o. + o.	w. + o.	nil + w.
80. Harwell (Yarwell?)	1 a. 3 r.	w. + o. + w.	o. + w.	o. + f.
81. Silverton (Sibberton: Thornhaugh?)	$19\frac{1}{2}$ a.	7 a: 2 w. + o. + o.	7 a: w. + o.	7 a: o. + f.
		7 a: w. +o. + w.	7 a: o. + w.	$5\frac{1}{2}$ a: w. + o.
		$5\frac{1}{2}$ a: w. + o. + f.	$5\frac{1}{2}$ a: w. + o. + f.	7 a: nil + w.
82. Stoke Doyle	17 a.	6 a: 2 w. + o. + o.	6 a: w. + o.	6 a: o. + f.
		6 a: w. + o. + w.	6 a: o. + w.	5 a: w. + o.
		5 a: 2 o. + w. + f.	5 a: w. + o. + f.	6 a: nil + w.
83. Northawe (Benefield)	3 a.	2 o. + w. + f.	w. + o. + f.	w. + o.
84. Walyle (Welcot Hall: Southorpe?)	$3\frac{1}{2}$ a.	2 w. + o. + o.	w. + o.	nil + w.
85. Hale: Apethorpe	2 a.	2 w. + o. + o.	w. + o.	nil + w.
86. Fotheringhay	15 a.	2 o. + w. + f.	w. + o. + f.	w. + o.
87. Blatherwycke	$2\frac{1}{2}$ a.	2 w. + o. + o.	w. + o.	nil + w.
88. Wytinge (Wittering)	8 a.	2 parts 2 w. + o. + (w.)	2 parts o. + w.	2 parts o. + f.
		3 rd part f. + (o.)	3 rd part w. + o. + f.	3rd part w. + o.
89. Rushton	1 a.	o. + f.	w. + o. + f.	w. + o.
90. Rushton	1 r.	?	?	?
91. Gretton	1 a.	o.	w. + o.	nil + w.
92. Little Weldon	$1\frac{1}{2}$ r.	o.	w. + o.	nil + w.
93. Little Weldon	4 a. 1 r.	o.	w. + o.	
94. Little Weldon	8 a.	o. + w.	o. + w.	8 a: o. + f.
95. Little Weldon	6 a.	o.	w. + o.	$10\frac{1}{2}$ a: nil + w.
96. Great Oakley	10 a.	o.	w. + o.	nil + w.
97. Faxton	2 a. 1 r.	2 o. + w. + f.	w. + o. + f.	o.

APPENDIX III

NORTHAMPTONSHIRE ASSARTING IN THE LATER THIRTEENTH CENTURY

After the mid-century groups summarized in Appendix II above, the next detail for assarting begins with 56 H III (1271-72) (E 32/72) for Whittlewood and Salcey, (E 32/73) for Rockingham. Then there is a jump of some fifteen years to 14 Ed I (E32/76, Cliffe and Rockingham) and 15 Ed I (E32/76 and 77, Whittlewood and Salcey). The old assarts in these lists for Whittlewood and Salcey do not correspond to any units to be found in the 1250's, so in the following tabulation it is assumed that these are new assarts at a desultory pace over the 1260's and 1270's. For Rockingham Forest, on the other hand, many of the large number of assarts in the 1250's lists are still kept on the Regarders' rolls throughout the 1270's and 1280's. Whether these were exactly the same assarts is of course difficult to determine in all cases since acreages are often larger, perhaps indicating new additions. A close study of local records may clarify the continuity of assarting. Nevertheless a good many additional assarts since the 1250's and after 1272 are sufficiently clear to be extracted for the following table.

SALCEY FOREST

NAME	*1271-72*	*1286-87*
Burnewode		1 a.
Horton	4½ a.	2 a.
Wasseneye	4½ a.	

WHITTLEWOOD FOREST

Grafton Regis		1 a.
	1 a. 1 r.	1 a. 1 r.
	1 a.	8 a.
	—	1 r.
Wespery: Paulerspury	1½ a.	1½ a.
	8 a. 1 r.	3 a.
Silverstone	2 a. ½ r.	—
	3 a.	
Wicken	2½ a.	
Puxley: Passenham	4	4 a.

WHITTLEWOOD FOREST cont'd

Ospery (East Perry?)		½a.
Hackleton	1 a. 1 r.	1 a. 1 r.
Alecote (Hulcote: Easton Neston)	1½a.	1½a.
Wootton	6 a.	
Tiffield	2 a.	2 a.
Kingshill	14 a.	14 a. (13 a.)
Alderton	1½a.	1½a.
Deanshanger	—	2 a.
Stoke (Bruerne?)	—	16 a. 1 r.
Wootton Fee	—	6 a.
Norton (Green's)	—	4 a.

ROCKINGHAM FOREST

NAME	*1271-72*	*1286-87*
Dingley	1 r.	
Desborough		½r.
Rushton		½a.
		2 a.
		8 a.
		1 a.
		4 a.
		6 a.
		2 a. 1 r.
Cottingham		2 a.
Little Weldon	2 a.	½a.
Deene	41 a.	
Deenethorpe		4 a. 1 r.
		4 a.
		4 a. 3 r.
Great Weldon	18 a.	38 a.
		3 a. 1 r.
		7 a.
Great Oakley		20 a.
		4 a.
Pilton		1 a.
Benefield	1 a. 1 r.	½a.
		½a.
		½a.
		½a.
		3 a.
		½a.
		1 a.
Linsdon (Lynn Wood: Blatherwycke?)		2 a.
		2 a.
		7 a.
Sudborough		50 a.
		4 a.
		10 a.

ROCKINGHAM FOREST cont'd		
NAME	*1271-72*	*1286-87*
Stanion	1 a.	1 a.
		1 r.
		1 a.
Little Oakley		1 a.
		1 a.
Aldwinkle, All Saints & St. Peter	1/2 r.	
Silverstone (Silbberton?)		11 1/2 a.
Laxton	1 1/2 a.	
Northawe (Benefield)	1/2 a.	
	1/2 a.	
	1/2 a.	
Wytinge (Wittering)		2 a.
Blatherwycke	4 a.	
	14 a.	5 1/2 a.
Cokefield		15 a.
Thornhawe		2 1/2 a.
Berford		2 a.
Rising Bridge: Geddington	15 a.	

APPENDIX IV

RENT AND SOWING OF THE WASTE IN THE FIRST HALF OF THE FOURTEENTH CENTURY

While fines for encroachment on waste are to be found in the earliest extant Forest Proceedings for Northants, these fines remained small and irregular and not obviously associated with the use of waste for pasture or assarting. Only from late in the reign of Edward I does the crown seem to have administered waste with the same efficiency that assarts had been administered over the previous century. In a document dated 12th November, 1305 (E32/85), and entitled Rents of Waste in Cliffe Forest, this new policy is first seen. Rent of waste in the remaining bailiwicks of Rockingham is recorded under the date 8th November, 1337 (E32/101). Rent of waste in Salcey and Whittlewood is first found in 1337 (E32/101, 10-11 Ed III).

Unlike assarting policy of previous generations, there is nothing in these first rental contracts to suggest that the waste had to be sown. Permission was given "to ditch, hedge and according to the assize of the forest to enclose, assart and cultivate." When assarting eventually took place, as was apparently the case for almost all the rented waste, the familiar Regarders of the Assarts came on the scene. These have left us a useful series of records beginning with E32/108 (for Salcey and Whittlewood, 1345-46), and E32/100 (Rockingham, 25th March 1334 ff.). E32/115 continues the Salcey and Whittlewood information for 1348-49. E32/106 and 110 has information upon use of rented waste in Rockingham over the late 1340's.

For the following tabulation properties are simply listed by numbers to correspond with appearance in the records rather than attempting to describe the exceptional detail given in these records for the location of the rented wastes. That is to say, the wastes were in the heart of the forests rather than in actual villages (although for Salcey and Whittlewood the waste was said to pertain to such and such a village) and given descriptive names from parts of the forest that could very likely be traced with local study.

TABLE A

RENT AND SOWING OF THE WASTE IN SALCEY AND WHITTLEWOOD

Entry No.	*Acreage*	*Rented* Date	Rent per Acre	Entry fine per Acre	*First Sown* Date	Grain
Salcey						
1.	60½ a.	1337-38	4 d.	12 d.	1343-44	o.
2.	32 a.	1337-38	4 d.	12 d.	1343-44	o.
	25 a.	1337-38	4 d.	12 d.	1343-44	o.
	3 a.	1337-38	4 d.	12 d.	1343-44	o.
3.	11½ a.	1337-38	4 d.	12 d.	1343-44	o.
4.	8½ a.	1337-38	4 d.	12 d.	1343-44	o.
	10 a.	1337-38	4 d.	12 d.	1343-44	o.
5.	10 a.	1337-38	4 d.	12 d.	1343-45	o.
6.	7 a.	1345-46			1345-46	?
7.	22 a.	1299-1300			1299-1300	w + o + f.
	10 a.	1299-1300			1299-1300	w + o + f.
	10 a.	1299-1300			1299-1300	w + o + f.
8.	5 a.	1299-1300			1299-1300	w + o + f.
9.	10 a.	1299-1300			1299-1300	o.
10.	8½ a.	1299-1300			1299-1300	?
11.	(2)	1299-1300			1299-1300	?
12.	8½ a.	1299-1300			1299-1300	o.
	5½ a.	1299-1300			1299-1300	o.
	10 a.	1299-1300			1299-1300	o.
13.	21 a.	1299-1300			1299-1300	o.
14.	23 a. 1 r.	1299-1300			1299-1300	?
15.	21 a.	1299-1300			1299-1300	?
16.	11 a.	1299-1300			1299-1300	?
17.	10 a.	1299-1300			1299-1300	o.
18.	14 a.	1299-1300			1299-1300	o.
19.	32 a.	1299-1300			1299-1300	o.
20.	20½ a.	1299-1300			1299-1300	o.
Whittlewood						
1.	40 a.	1337-38	4 d.	12 d.	1343-44	o.
2.	17½ a.	1337-38	4 d.	12 d.	1343-44	o.
3.	26 a.	1337-38	4 d.	12 d.	1343-44	o.
4.	213 a.	1337-38	4 d.	12 d.	1343-44	?
5	90 a. 3 r.	1337-38	4 d.	12 d.	1343-44	?
6.	7½ a.	1337-38	4 d.	12 d.	1336-37	?
7.	7½ a.	1298-99	—	—	1298-99	o.
8.	22 a.	1298-99	—	—	1298-99	o.
9.	28½ a. 1 r.	1298-99	—	—	1298-99	o.
10.	32 a. ½ r.	1298-99	—	—	1298-99	o.
11.	7 a.	1298-99	—	—	1298-99	?
12.	3½ a.	1298-99	—	—	1298-99	?
13.	6 a.	1298-99	—	—	1298-99	?
14.	12½ a. ¼ r.	1298-99	—	—	1298-99	?
15.	13 a.	1298-99	—	—	1298-99	?
16.	11 a.	?	—	—	Not sown	
17.	3 a.	?	—	—	Not sown	

TABLE A cont'd

Note: — in E32/115, 12th March 1348, further assarts are indicated pertaining to the following villages.

Villages	*Acrage*	Date	*Rented* Rent per Acre	Entry fine per Acre	*First Sown* Date	Grain
Piddington	10 a.	?	—	—	1299-1300	?
Preston (Deanery)	1 a. 1 1/2 r.	1282-83	—	—	1299-1300	?
Horton	2 a.	1282-83	—	—	1299-1300	?
Burnewode	11 1/2 a.	1282-83	—	—	1299-1300	?
(Passenham)	19 a.	not known	—	—	1301-02	?
Silverstone	1 a. +.	1336-37	—	—	1338-39	?
	1 a +.	(enclosed)				
	2 a +.					
	3 a +.					
	2 a +.					
	2 a +.					

TABLE B

WASTE RENTALS IN ROCKINGHAM FOREST

Entry No. (E32/85)	*Acreage*	Date	*Rented* Rented per Acre	Entry Fine per Acre
1.	20 a. 3 r. 10 p.	1300	6 d.	18 d.
2.	24 a. 3 1/2 r. 7 p.	1300	4 d.	18 d.
3.	3 a. 1 r.	1301	4 d.	12 d.
4.	18 a. 3 r. 6 p.	1305	4 d.	18 d.
5.	65 1/2 a. 12 p.	1305	4 d.	24 d.
6.	47 a. 1 1/2 r.	1305	4 d.	12 d.
7.	15 1/2 a. 8 p.	1305	4 d.	4 d.
8.	10 a. 3 r. 16 p.	1305	2 d.	4 d.
9.	147 1/2 a. 1/2 r. 17 1/2 p.	1305	4 d.	12 d.
10.	49 a. 1 1/2 r. 18 p.	1305	3 d.	8 d.
11.	29 a. 3 r.	1305	2 d.	4 d.
12.	20 a. 1 r.	1305	3 d	6 d.
13.	11 1/2 a. 1/2 r. 16 p.	1305	4 d.	18 d.
14.	4 a. 1 1/2 r. 6 p.	1305	2 d.	6 d.
15.	1 1/2 a.	1305	4 d.	12 d.
(E32/101)				
1.	20 a.	1337	4 d.	12 d.
2.	20 a.	1337	4 d.	12 d.
3.	8 a.	1337	4 d.	12 d.
4.	8 1/2 a.	1337	4 d.	12 d.
5.	8 1/2 a.	1337	4 d.	12 d.
6.	2 a.	1337	4 d.	12 d.

TABLE B cont'd

Entry No.	*Acreage*	Date	*Rented* Acre	per Acre
(E32/101) cont'd.				
7.	7 a.	1337	4 d.	12 d.
8.	4 a.	1337	4 d.	12 d.
8a.	1½ a. 1 r.	1337	4 d.	12 d.
9.	12 a.	1337	4 d.	12 d.
10.	6 a.	1337	4 d.	12 d.
11.	31½ a.	1337	4 d.	12 d.
12.	10 a.	1337	4 d.	12 d.
13.	7 a.	1337	4 d.	12 d.
14.	4 a.	1337	4 d.	12 d.
15.	4 a.	1337	4 d.	12 d.
16.	4 a.	1337	4 d.	12 d.
17.	5 a.	1337	4 d.	12 d.
18.	6½ a.	1337	4 d.	12 d.
19.	21 a.	1337	4 d.	12 d.
20.	3½ a.	1337	4 d.	12 d.
21.	3½ a.	1337	4 d.	12 d.
22.	5 a.	1337	4 d.	12 d.
23.	5 a.	1337	4 d.	12 d.
24.	12½ a.	1337	4 d.	12 d.
25.	4 a.	1337	4 d.	12 d.
26.	2 a.	1337	4 d.	12 d.
27.	5 a.	1337	4 d.	12 d.
28.	16 a.	1337	4 d.	12 d.
29.	40 a.	1337	4 d.	12 d.
30.	(5½ a.)	1337	4 d.	12 d.
31.	30 a.	1337	4 d.	12 d.
32.	6 a.	1337	4 d.	12 d.
33.	63 a.	1337	4 d.	12 d.
34.	94 a.	1337	4 d.	12 d.
35.	15 a.	1337	4 d.	12 d.

TABLE C

SOWING OF THE WASTE IN ROCKINGHAM FOREST

Entry No.	*Acreage*	*E32/100*	*E32/106*	*E32/110*
1.	10 a.	w. + 2 o. + frisc'	w. + o.	w. + o.
2.	2 1/2 a.	frisc'	frisc'	frisc'
3.	8 a.	frisc'	frisc'	frisc'
4.	10 a.	subbosco	subbosco	subbosco
5.	6 a.	3 w. + 3 o.	w. + o.	w. + o.
6.	18 a.	3 w. + 3 o.	w. + o.	w. + o.
7.	2 a.	3 w. + 3 o.	(w). + o.	w. + o.
8.	2 a.	3 w. + 3 o.	w. + o.	2 w. + o.
9.	12 a.	frisc'	frisc'	frisc'
10.	12 a.	frisc'	frisc'	frisc'
11.	1/2 a.	?	w. + o.	?
12.	16 1/2 a.	3 w. + 3 o.	2 o.	w. + o.
13.	60 a.	3 w. + 3 o.	2 o.	w. + o.
14.	5 a.	3 w. + 3 o.	o.	o.
15.	80 a.	w. (15 a.) + peas + o. in equal portions + f. + frisc'	w. (15 a.) + peas + o. in equal portions + f. + frisc'	same
16.	5 a.	frisc'	frisc'	frisc'
17.	8 1/2 a.	3 w. + 3 o.	peas + o.	w.
18.	12 a.	3 w. + 3 o.	2 o.	o.
19.	7 a.	frisc'	frisc'	w.
20.	13 a.	w.	w. + o.	o.
21.	60 a.	3 w. + 3 o.	w. + o.	w. (+?)
22.	20 a.	3 w. + 3 o.	2 o.	o.
23.	49 a.	3 w. + 3 o.	w. + 2 o.	w. (+?)
24.	40 a.	3 w. + 3 o.	w. + o.	?
25.	9 a.	3 w. + 3 o.	peas + o.	w.
26.	10 a.	3 w. + 3 o.	2 o.	w.
27.	2 a.	3 w. + 3 o.	2 o.	peas
28.	4 a.	3 w. + 3 o.	w. + o.	o.

TABLE C cont'd

Entry No.	*Acreage*	*E32/100*	*E32/106*	*E32/110*
29.	5 a.	3 w. + 3 o.	o. + barley mixed	barley
30.	3 r.	frisc'	frisc'	frisc'
31.	12 a.	frisc'	frisc'	2 o.
32.	30 a.	3 w. + 3 o.	w. + o.	w.
33.	20 a.	3 w. + 3 o.	w. + o.	(w)
34.	50 a.	(3 w. + 3 o.)	w. + o.	o.
35.	2 a.	3 w. + 3 o.	w. + o.	w. + o.
36.	8 a.	subbosc	subbosc	subbosc
37.	12 a.	3 w. + 3 o.	w. + o.	o.
38.	15 a.	3 w. + 3 o.	w. + o.	w.
39.	15 a.	3 w. + 3 o.	?	w.
40.	4 a.	3 w. + 3 o.	2 o. + 2 o.	
			2a of subbosc	o.
41.	8 a.	3 w. + 3 o.	w. + o.	w.
42.	2$^1/_2$ a. 1 r.	3 w. + 3 o.	w. + o.	o.
43.	2$^1/_2$ a. 1 r.	3 w. + 3 o.	w. + o.	w.
44.	2$^1/_2$ a. 1 r.	3 w. + 3 o.	w. + o.	o.
45.	2$^1/_2$ a. 1 r.	3 w. + 3 o.	w. + o.	w.
46.	2$^1/_2$ a. 1 r.	3 w. + 3 o.	w. + o.	peas and oats mixed
47.	5 a.	3 w. + 3 o.	2 o.	?
48.	2 a.	3 w. + 3 o.	w. + o.	w.
49.	6 a.	3 o.	2 o.	w.
50.	30 a.	3 o.	2 o.	2 o.
51.	6 a.	3 o.	o.	w.
52.	6 a.	2 o.	2 o.	w.
53.	90 a.	w. + 3 o.	w. + o.	w.
54.	40 a.	w. + 2 o.	w. + o.	o.
55.	60 a.	nil	o.	w.
56.	20 a.	nil	o.	o.
57.	15 a.	w. + o.	?	o.
58.	60 a.	frisc'	frisc'	frisc'
59.	4 a.	3 o. + 3 w.	w. + o.	w.
60.	5 a.	3 o. + 3 w.	w. + o.	dredge

TABLE C cont'd

Entry No.	*Acreage*	*E32/100*	*E32/106*	*E32/110*
61.	5 a.	3 o. + 3 w.	w. + o.	w.
62.	15 a.	nil	o.	nil?
63.	5 a.	nil	nil	nil
64.	21 a.	3 o.	w. + o.	o.
65.	?	nil	nil	nil
66.	3 a.	nil	2 o.	2 a. — w.
				1 a. pasture
67.	3 a.	nil	o.	2 a. — o.
				1 a. pasture
68.	26 a.	nil	nil	nil
69.	1½ a.	nil	nil	nil
70.	5 a.	nil	o.	o.
71.	4½ a.	nil	nil	nil
72.	5 a.	nil	nil	nil
73.	(5) a.	nil	nil	nil
74.	5 a.	nil	nil	nil
75.	10 a.	nil	nil	nil
76.	7 a.	nil	nil	nil
77.	20 a.	2 o.	2 o.	o.
78.	8 a.	o.	w. + o.	w.
79.	20 a.	3 o.	2 o.	o.
80.	2 a.	3 o.	w. + o.	?
81.	8 a.	3 o.	2 o.	w.
82.	8 a.	3 o.	w. + o.	w.
83.	6 a.	3 o.	2 o.	o.
84.	2 a.	nil	2 o.	w.
85.	12 a.	nil	8 a. — 2 o.	8 a. — w.
			4 a. — frisc'	4 a. — frisc'
86.	6 a.	nil	2 a. — pasture	4 a. — o.
			4 a. — 2 o.	2 a. — pasture
87.	6 a.	2 o.	2 o.	w.
88.	6 a.	2 o.	2 o.	w.

APPENDIX V

INTRODUCTION

Geographically the royal forest of the Buckinghamshire Forest Proceedings are simply an extension of the Northants forests of Salcey and Whittlewood. Assart lists for the early thirteenth century show activity scattered as widely throughout the villages of Stotfold Hundred below Whittlewood as in the Northants region of this forest. About Salcey (*Sauceia* in the Bucks records), however, there was more activity than in Northants, extending beyond the Bucks Hundred of Bunsty to embrace much of the whole northern 'peninsula' of the county.

Since the chronology of the five assart lists extant for the early thirteenth century is not entirely clear, these assarts have not been gathered together in one table (A) under entries common to various properties. In any case, the manner of listing crops sown seems to suggest a more uniform rotation system for the assarts of Bucks than those of Northants. Totals of villages and hamlets, acres, and crops represented in these lists are as follows:

	Villages	*Acreage*	*Crops*
First List:	16	146 a. 3 r.	51 wheat
Second List:	18	211 a. 1 r.	60 oats
Third List:	14	124 a. 1 r.	35 wheat, 1 oat, 5 fallow
Fourth List:	8	71 a. 2 r.	2 wheat, 19 oats
Fifth List:	12	138 a. 3 r.	31 oats

Until the chronology of these lists can be more firmly established it is not possible to say whether wheat and oat-sown assarts ought to be added to give the total assart figure for the village.

Very likely the variety of amounts in the lists may at least be taken as a rough indication of the new assarting fever at this time.

Table B presents the good assart list available for several years in the 1250's. Again the manner of recording the assart differs from that of the Regarders of Northants in that no data were recorded for crops of the previous years (that is, since the last Regard), and the general terms 'winter' and 'spring' sowing were employed. Furthermore, the decayed condition of the manuscript makes identification of properties difficult. The rotation system does seem to have followed the same standard sequence as in Northants, although it has not been reconstructed here because of the above problems of identification. The total data for sowing from these lists are as follows:

	Villages	Acreage	Crops
Table B. 1249-50:	8	291 a. 3½ r.	37 wheat 34 oats
Table B. 1252-53:	43 (assart units)	253 a. 3½ r. +	34 wheat 30 oats
Table B. 1254-55:	6 +	245 a. 2½ r.	30 wheat 33 oats

APPENDIX V

ASSARTS IN THE ROYAL FORESTS OF BUCKINGHAMSHIRE IN THE THIRTEENTH CENTURY

E32/249, membranes 18-20

TABLE A

THE EARLY THIRTEENTH CENTURY

First List

Saucey Forest

Entry No.	*Place*	*Acreage*	*Crops*
1.	Abinton (Lavendon)	3 r.	w.
2.	Lavendon	½ a.	w.
3.	Lavendon	½ a.	w.
4.	Weston	½ a.	w.
5.	Weston	½ a.	w.
6.	Weston	½ a.	w.
7.	Weston	1 r.	w.
8.	Weston	1½ a.	w.
9.	Weston	1 r.	w.
10.	Weston	1 r.	w.
11.	Ravenstone	1 a.	w.
12.	Ravenstone	3 r.	w.
13.	Ravenstone	1 a. 1 r.	w.
14.	Ravenstone	½ a.	w.
15.	Ravenstone	13 a.	w.
16.	Ravenstone	½ a.	w.
17.	Ravenstone	1 r.	w.
18.	Ravenstone	6 a.	w.
19.	Ravenstone	r.	w.
20.	Ravenstone	1 r.	w.
21.	Ravenstone	1½ a.	w.
22.	Ravenstone	1 r.	w.
23.	Hoteleya (Hoo Wood: Gayhurst?)	1 r.	w.

TABLE A cont'd

24.	Stoke (Goldington)	2 a.	w.
25.	Lathbury	$2^1/_2$ a.	w.
26.	Lathbury	$2^1/_2$ a.	w.
27.	Stoking Green (Hanslope)	6 a.	w.
28.	Lathbury	6 a.	w.
29.	Linford Great	4 a.	w.
30.	Haversham	$12^1/_2$ a.	w.
31.	Hanslope	$33^1/_2$ a.	w.
32.	Hanslope	1 a.	w.
33.	Hanslope	$^1/_2$ a.	w.
34.	Hanslope	1 r.	w.
35.	Hanslope	$4^1/_2$ a.	w.
36.	Hanslope	1 r.	w.
37.	Hanslope	$^1/_2$ a.	w.
38.	Hanslope	3 r.	w.
39.	Hanslope	$1^1/_2$ a.	w.
40.	Hanslope	4 a.	w.
41.	Hanslope	1 a.	w.
42.	Hanslope	3 a.	w.
43.	Hanslope	3 r.	w.
44.	Hanslope	1 a.	w.
45.	Hanslope	2 a.	w.

Whittlewood Forest

46.	Hanslope	3 a.	w.
47.	Hanslope	7 a.	w.
48.	Akeley	10 a.	w.
49.	Westbury	$^1/_2$ a.	w.
50.	Dadford	$2^1/_2$ a.	w.
51.	(Evershaw in Biddlesden)	$^1/_2$ a.	w.

Second List

Saucey Forest

Entry No.	*Place*	*Acreage*	*Crops*
1.	Lavendon	$2^1/_2$ a.	o.
2.	Lavendon	3 a.	o.
3.	Lavendon	$^1/_2$ a.	o.
4.	Lavendon	3 r.	o.
5.	Olney	25 a.	o.
6.	Olney	$1^1/_2$ a.	o.

TABLE A cont'd

7.	Weston (Underwood)	1 r.	o.
8.	Weston (Underwood)	1 a. 3 r.	o.
9	Weston (Underwood)	1 r.	o.
10.	Weston (Underwood)	1 r.	o.
11.	Weston (Underwood)	3 r.	o.
12.	Weston (Underwood)	2 a.	o.
13.	Weston (Underwood)	1 r.	o.
14.	Weston (Underwood)	3 a.	o.
15.	Ravenstone	1 r.	o.
16.	Ravenstone	1 r.	o.
17.	Ravenstone	1 r.	o.
18.	Ravenstone	3 r.	o.
19.	Ravenstone	1 a. 1 r.	o.
20.	Ravenstone	1 r.	o.
21.	Ravenstone	1/2 a.	o.
22.	Ravenstone	1/2 a.	o.
23.	Ravenstone	1 r.	o.
24.	Ravenstone	1 a.	o.
25.	Ravenstone	13 a.	o.
26.	Hoteleya (Hoo Wood: Gayhurst)	6 a.	o.
27.	Hoteleya (Hoo Wood: Gayhurst)	1 r.	o.
28.	Stoke Goldington	2 a.	o.
29.	Stoke Goldington	1 r.	o.
30.	Lathbury	4 a.	o.
31.	Lathbury	2 1/2 a.	o.
32.	Gayhurst	2 a.	o.
33.	Stoking Green (Hanslope)	7 a.	o.
34.	Lathbury	7 a.	o.
35.	Lathbury	6 a.	o.
36.	(Haversham)	12 1/2 a.	o.
37.	Hanslope	32 1/2 a.	( )
38.	Hanslope	1/2 a.	o.
39.	Hanslope	1 r.	o.
40.	Hanslope	4 1/2 a.	o.
41.	Hanslope	1 r.	o.
42.	Hanslope	5 r.	o.

TABLE A cont'd

43.	Hanslope	3 r	o.
44.	Hanslope	1 1/2 a.	o.
45.	Hanslope	1/2 a.	o.
46.	Hanslope	4 a.	o.
47.	Hanslope	1 a.	o.
48.	Hanslope	3 a.	o.
49.	Hanslope	3 r.	o.
50.	Hanslope	2 a.	o.
51.	Hanslope	1 a.	o.
Whittlewood			
52.	Leckhampstead	1 1/2 a.	o.
53.	Leckhampstead	5 a.	o.
54.	Lillingstone	1 r.	o.
55.	Lillingstone	24 a.	o.
56.	Akeley	8 a.	o.
57.	Akeley	1 a. 3 r.	o.
58.	Akeley	1/2 a.	o.
59.	Dadford	2 1/2 a.	o.
60.	Dadford	1 1/2 a.	o.
61.	(Evershaw?)	2 a.	o.

Third List

Saucey Forest

Entry No.	*Place*	*Acreage*	*Crops*
1.	Habinton	3 r.	w.
2.	Lavendon	1/2 a.	w.
3.	Lavendon	1 a. 1 r.	w.
4.	(Olney)	1 1/2 a.	w.
5.	Weston (Underwood)	3 r.	w.
6.	Weston	1/2 a.	w.
7.	Weston	3 r.	w.
8.	Weston	3 r.	o.
9.	Weston	1 r.	w.
10.	Weston	1 r.	w.
11.	Weston	1/2 a.	w.
12.	Ravenstone	1 r.	w.
13.	Ravenstone	3 r.	w.
14.	Ravenstone	1 a. 1 r.	w.
15.	Ravenstone	1/2 a.	w.
16.	Ravenstone	1 a.	w.
17.	Ravenstone	13 a.	w.
18.	Hoteleya (Hoo Wood: Gayhurst?)	1 r.	w.

TABLE A cont'd

19.	Hoteleya (Hoo Wood: Gayhurst?)	1 r.	w.
20.	Lathbury	2 1/2 a.	w.
21.	Lathbury	2 1/2 a.	w.
22.	Lathbury	2 1/2 a.	w.
23.	Stoking Green (Hanslope)	6 a.	w.
24.	Stoking Green (Hanslope)	6 a.	f.
25.	Linford (Gt.)	6 1/2 a.	w.
26.	Hanslope	32 1/2 a.	w.
27.	Hanslope	2 1/2 a.	w.
28.	Hanslope	1 a.	w.
29.	Hanslope	1/2 a.	w.
30.	Hanslope	1 a.	w.
31.	Hanslope	4 1/2 a.	w.
32.	Hanslope	1/2 a.	w.
33.	Hanslope	3 a.	w.
34.	Hanslope	3 r.	f.
35.	Hanslope	1 1/2 a.	f.
36.	Hanslope	1 a.	w.
Whittlewood Forest			
37.	Leckhampstead	1 1/2 a.	(f)
38.	Leckhampstead	5 a.	(f)
39.	Lillingstone	1 r.	w.
40.	Akeley	12 a.	w.
41.	Westpery (Paulerspury: Northants?)	2 a.	w.

Fourth List

Saucey Forest

Entry No.	*Place*	*Acreage*	*Crops*
* 1.	Lavendon	1 r.	w.
* 2.	Padbury	10 r.	w.
* 3.	Padbury	20 a.	o.
4.	(Hanslope)	1/2 a.	o.
5.	Hanslope	3 r.	o.
6.	Hanslope	1/2 a.	o.
7.	Hanslope	1 a.	o.
8.	Hanslope	1 a.	o.
9.	Hanslope	1 1/2 a.	o.
10.	Hanslope	3 a.	o.
11.	Hanslope	3 r.	o.
12.	Hanslope	1 a.	o.
13.	Hanslope	2 1/2 a.	o.

* These 3 entries are designated as "new assarts", all other entries in these lists appear to be "old assarts".

TABLE A cont'd

Whittlewood

14.	[Leckhamptstead]	3 a.	o.
15.	Lillingstone	½ a.	o.
16.	Lillingstone	12 a.	o.
17.	Akeley	10 a.	o.
18.	Akeley	1 a. 3 r.	o.
19.	Doddford (Dadford)	2 a.	o.
20.	Doddford (Dadford)	1½ a.	o.
21.	(Evershaw)?	1½ a.	o.

Fifth List

Saucey Forest

1.	Lavendon	2½ a.	o.
2.	Lavendon	3 a.	o.
3.	Lavendon	½ a.	o.
4.	Olney	25 a.	o.
5.	Weston (Underwood)	1 r.	o.
6.	Weston (Underwood)	3 a.	o.
7.	Weston (Underwood)	2 a.	o.
8.	Weston (Underwood)	3 a.	o.
9.	Ravenstone	4 r.	o.
10.	Ravenstone	½ a.	o.
11.	Ravenstone	6 a.	o.
12.	Ravenstone	½ a.	o.
13.	Ravenstone	3 r.	o.
14.	Ravenstone	1 a. 1 r.	o.
15.	Ravenstone	½ a.	o.
16.	Ravenstone	½ a.	o.
17.	Ravenstone	1 a.	o.
18.	Ravenstone	½ a.	o.
19.	Ravenstone	1 a.	o.
20.	Ravenstone	3 r.	o.
21.	Ravenstone	13 a.	o.
22.	Hoteleya (Hoo Wood: Gayhurst?)	6 a.	o.
23.	Stoke (Goldington)	2 a.	o.
24.	Stoke (Goldington)	1 r.	o.
25.	Lathbury	4 a.	o.
26.	Gayhurst	2 a.	o.
27.	Stoking Green (Hanslope)	6 a.	o.
28.	Lathbury	6 a.	o.
29.	(Lathbury)	1 a.	o.
30.	(Haversham)	12½ a.	o.
31.	Hanslope	32½ a.	o.

ASSARTS IN THE ROYAL FORESTS OF BUCKINGHAMSHIRE IN THE MID THIRTEENTH CENTURY

TABLE B

1249-50 (34 H III)

Entry No.	*Place*	*Acreage and Crops*	*Value (Fine)*
Whittlewood			
1.	Stoke (Morewell?)	11 a 1 r. w.*	
		11 a. 1 r: o.	35s. 10d.
2.	Horton	1 a 1 r: w.	15d.
3.	Cadinton	7 a: w.	
	(Warrington?)	13 a: o.	13s. 6d.
4.	Hanslope	1 a: w.	
		14 a: o.	8s.
5.	Hanslope	3 a. 1 r: w.	
		6½ a. 1 r: o.	6s. 4d.
6.	Hanslope	2½ a: o.	15d.
7.	Hanslope	1 a: w.	
		14 a: o.	8s.
8.	Hanslope	3 a: w.	
		7 a: o.	6s. 6d.
9	Hanslope	2 a: o.	
		13 a: w.	8s. 6d.
10.	Hanslope	2 a: w.	
		4 a: o.	4s.
11.	Hanslope	2½ a: o.	15d.
12.	Hanslope	2 a: w.	
		3 r: o.	23s. 4d. ob.
13.	Hanslope	½ a: w.	
		½ r: o.	3d. ob. q.
14.	Hanslope	½ a: w.	
		1 r: o.	7d. ob.
15.	Hanslope	7 a: w.	
		14 a. 1 r: o.	14s. 3d. ob.
16.	Hanslope	1 r: w.	
		½ a: o.	6d.
17.	Hanslope	1 r: o.	3d. ob.
18.	Hanslope	2½ a: w.	2s. 6d.
19.	Hanslope	1 r: w.	
		1 r: o.	4d. ob.
20.	Hanslope	½ a: o.	3d.
21.	Hanslope	½ a: w.	
		½ a: o.	9d.
22.	Hanslope	½ a: o.	3d.

* Although wheat and oats are employed in the table, the manuscript refers only to winter and summer sowings.

TABLE B cont'd

1249-50 (34 H III)

Entry No.	Place	Acreage and Crops	Value
23.	Hanslope	1/2 a: o.	3d.
24.	Hanslope	1/2 r: o.	3d. q.
25.	Hanslope	1 1/2 r: o.	2d. q.
26.	Leckhampstead	4 a: w.	
		9 a: o.	8s. 6d.
27.	Leckhampstead	7 a: w.	
		14 a: o.	14s.
28.	Foscott	3 a: o.	18d.
29.	Moreton (Maids?)	1 r: o.	3d. ob.
30.	( )	20 a: w.	
		28 1/2 a: o.	39s. 6d.
31.	Lillingstone?	5 a: w.	
		10 1/2 a: o.	10s. 3d.
32.	Lillingstone?	2 a: w.	
		5 a: o.	5s.
33.	Lillingstone?	3 r: w.	
		1 1/2 a: o.	18d.
34.	Lillingstone?	3 a. 1/2 r: w.	
		6 a: o.	6s. 3. ob.
35.	Lillingstone?	1 1/2 a: o.	9d.
36.	Lillingstone?	5 1/2 a: w.	
		5 a: o.	8s.
37.	Lillingstone?	1 1/2 a: w.	
		3 r: o.	2s. 3d. ob.
38.	Lillingstone?	1/2 a: w.	
		(1/2 a?) 1/2 r: o.	15d.
39.	Lillingstone?	3 r: o.	4d. ob.

1252-53 (37 H. III)

Entry No.	Place	Acreage and Crops	Value
1.		2 a. 1 r: w.	
		2 a. 1 r. o.	3s. 4d. ob.
2.		1 a. 1 r: o.	7d. ob.
3.		8 a: w.	
		12 a: o.	14s.
4.		4 a: w.	
		6 a: o.	7s.
5.		1 a: w.	
		1 1/2 a: o.	21d.
6.		5 a: w.	
		10 a: o.	10s.
7.		7 a: w.	
		18 a: o.	16s.
8.		3 a: w.	
		3 a: o.	4s. 6d.
9.		2 1/2 a: w.	2s. 6d.

TABLE B cont'd

1252-53 (37 H. III)

Entry No.	*Place*	*Acreage and Crops*	*Value*
10.		2 a: w.	
		3 r: o.	2s. 4d. ob.
11.		1½ r: o.	2d. q.
12.		½ a: w.	
		1 r: o.	7d. ob.
13.		7 a: w.	
		14 a: o.	14s.
14.		1 r: w.	
		½ a: o.	6d.
15.		1 r: w.	3d.
16.		2½ r: w.	2s. 6d.
17.		½ a: o.	3d.
18.		½ a: w.	3d.
19.		½ a: w.	
		3 r: o.	10d. ob.
20		2 a: w.	
		2 a: o.	3s.
21.		½ a: w.	6d.
22.		½ a: w.	
		3 r: o.	10d. ob.
23.		½ a: w.	6d.
24.		½ a: w.	6d.
25.		½ r: o.	3d. q.
26.		1½ r: o.	2d. q.
27.		4 a: w.	
		9 a: o.	8s. 6d.
28.		7 a: w.	
		14 a: o.	14s.
29.		3 a: w.	18d.
30.		( ) w.	1d. ob.
31.		( ) w. ( ) o.	39s.
32.		3r: o.	3d. ob.
33.		5a: w.; 10½ a: o.	10s. 3d.
34.		( ) w.	4s. 6d.
		5 a: o.	
35.	(Bernwood)	3 r: w.	
		1 a. 1 r: o.	16d. ob.
36.		8 a: w.	
		½ a. ½ r: o.	7s. 3d. ob. q.
37.		1½ a. ½ r: o.	9d. ob. q.
38.		1½ a. ½ r: o.	9d. ob. q.
39.		1½ a. ½ r: o.	9d. ob. q.
40.		½ a: w.	
		½ a. ½ r: o.	9d. ob. q.
41.		1½ a: o.	9d.
42.		3 r: o.	4d. ob.

TABLE B

1254-55 (39 H. III)

Entry No.	*Place**	*Acreage and Crops*	*Value*
1.		2 a. + 1 r: w.	
		2 a. + 1 r: o.	3s. 4d.
2.		1/2 a: w.	
		3 r: o.	10d. ob.
3.		6 1/2 a. + 1/3 part of 1/2 a.	3s. 4d.
4.		6 1/2 a. + 1/3 part of 1/2 a.	3s. 4d.
5.		6 1/2 a. + 1/3 part of 1/2 a.	3s. 4d.
6.		3 1/2 a: w; 6 1/2 a: o.	6s. 4d.
7.		2 1/2 a: o.	15d.
8.		5 a: w.	
		10 a: o.	10s.
9.		4 a: w.	
		6 a: o.	7s.
10.		6 a: w.	
		9 a: o.	10s. 6d.
11.		3 a: w.	
		3 a: o.	4s. 6d.
12.		2 1/2 a: w.	2s. 6d.
13.		1 1/2 a: w.	
		1 1/2 a. + 1 r: o.	2s. 3d.
14.		1 a. 1/2 r: o.	3d. ob. q.
15.		1/2 a: w.	
		1 r: o.	7d. ob.
16.		7 a: w.	
		14 a: o.	14s.
17.		1/2 a: w.	
		1 r: o.	7d. ob.
18.		1 r: w.	2d.
19.		( ) w.	
		1 a: o.	2s.
20.		1/2 a: o.	3d.
21.		1/2 a: w.	
		1/2 a: o.	9d. ob.
22.		1 a: w.	
		3 a: o.	2s. 6d.
23.		1/2 a: w.	6d.
24.		1/2 a: w.	
		3 r: o.	10d. ob.
25.		1/2 a: w.	6d.
26.		1/2 a: w.	6d.
27.		1/2 r: o.	3d. q.
28.		1 1/2 r: o	2d. q.
29.	Leckhampstead	4 a: w.	
		9 a: o.	8s. 6d.
30.		7 a: w.	
		14 a: o.	14s.
31.	Foscott	3 a: w.	3s.

* The left margin, indicating places assarted, is decayed away for the great part of this folio, so that places cannot be indicated for much of Table B (1252-53) (1254-55).

TABLE B cont'd

1254-55 (39 H. III)

Entry No.	*Place*	*Acreage and Crops*	*Value*
32.	Moreton (Maids)	1 r: o.	3d.
33.	Akeley	20 a: w. 38½ a: o.	39s. 3d.
34.	Akeley	3 r: o.	4d. ob.
35.	Lillingstone	2½ a: w. 5 a: o.	5s.
36.	Lillingstone	½ a: w. ½ a: o.	9d.
37.	Lillingstone	½ a: w. ½ a: o.	9d.
38.	Lillingstone	3 a: w. 3 a: o. + 1 (?)	4s. 7d. ob.
39.	Lillingstone	2½ a: w. 2½ a: o.	3s. 9d. ob.
40.	Lillingstone	1 a: w. ½ a. ½ r: o.	15d. ob. q.
41.	Lillingstone	½ a: w. 1 a. ½ r: o.	12d. ob. q.
42.	Westbury	½ r: w. 1 a. 3 r: o.	14d. q.

ASSARTS IN BERNWOOD FOREST
IN THE MID THIRTEENTH CENTURY

TABLE C

Entry No.	*Place*	*1249-1250* *Acreage and Crop*	*Value*	*1252-1253* *Acreage and Crop*	*Value*	*1254-1255* *Acreage and Crop*	*Value*
1.	Be: nwood	1 a: w.	12d.	1 r: o.	3d.	1 r: o.	3d.
2.	Bernwood	$3^1/_2$ a. 1 r: w.	3s. 9d.	$3^1/_2$ a. 1 r: o.	22d. ob	3 a. 3 r: o.	22d. ob
3.	Bernwood	5 a: w.		3 a: w.			
		4 a: o.	7s.	5 a: o.	6s. 6d.	5 a: o.	2s. 6d.
4.	Bernwood	1 r: w.	3d.	1 r: o.	3d. ob		
5.	Bernwood	$3^1/_2$ a: w.	3s. 6d.	11 a: o.	5s. 6d.	3 a: w.	3s.
						2 a: o.	12d.
6.	Bernwood			15 a: o.	7s. 6d.	8 a: w.	
						7 a: o.	11s. 6d.
7.	Bernwood			$1^1/_2$ a: o.	9d.		

APPENDIX VI

Introduction

As may be seen in the following tables assarting was widely spread throughout Huntingdonshire too in the early thirteenth century. Table A represents 522 acres 1/2 rod in 18 villages. Overshadowed all along the north and west by the powerful lordships of fen monasteries, with forest liberties reaching back long before the thirteenth century, much of this country was exempted from the purview of the royal Regarders. Only in the occasional entry, as with the 300 acres of the Abbot of Ely at Somersham, do we find indications of the immensity of the acres assarted (or available to assarts) by these monasteries.

Table B (37 acres 3 1/2 rods in 59 villages) shows that, unlike Northamptonshire, active new assarting at Hunts was small around the mid thirteenth century. Of the new assarts regarded in 1286 (Table C: 144 acres and 1 1/4 rood: 16 villages) the acreage size is much smaller than the assarts near the beginning of the century, and of the larger assarts in 1286, it is noteworthy that the 35 acres of Kingsdelf are in meadow and of the 60 acres of "Lymmynges" only 16 are sown, and these with oats.

TABLE A

ASSARTS OF HUNTINGDONSHIRE IN EARLY THIRTEENTH CENTURY

E32/248

Entry No.	*Place*	*Acreage*	*Corn*	*Value*
1.	Dillington (Gt. Staughton)	15 a.	o.	30s.
2.	Dillington (Gt. Staughton)	5 a.	not sown	
3.	Buckden	1 a.	w. + o.	4s.
4.	Perry	1 a.	o.	5s.
5.	Perry	2 a.	w. + o.	6s. 8d.
6.	Perry	large assart		
7.	Ellington	8½ a.	w. + o.	17s.
8.	Ellington	2 a.	w. + o.	4s.
9.	Ellington	9 a.	?	?
10.	Easton	1½ a.	o.	3s.
11.	Grafham	½ a.	w.	18d.
12.	Hail Weston	8 a.	w. + o.	13s. 4d.
13.	Alconbury	53 a. 3 r.	w. + o.	113s. 4d.
14.	Alconbury	6 a. ½ r.	o.	13s. 4d.
15.	Stukeley	3 a. 1 r.	w. ord + o.	13s. 4d.
16.	Honour of Hunts	15 a.	o.	30s.
17.	Honour of Hunts	15 a.	f.	f.

18.	Ripton (Abbots)	8 a.	o.	13s. 4d.
19.	Ripton (Abbots)	10 a.	w. + o.	30s.
20.	Stukeley	9 a.	w. + o.	18s.
21.	Stukeley	7 a.	w.	14s. 1d.
22.	Walton	2 a.	o. (1 a.) + f. (1 a.)	2s.
23.	Upton	1 a.	w.	2s.
24.	Coppingford	1 a.	w.	2s.
25.	Washingley	(7½ a.)	o.	10s.
26.	Washingley	5 a.	not sown	
27.	Washingley	3 a. 3 r.	o. + w.	4s.
28.	Sawtry	21 a. 1 r.	w.	53s.
29.	(Hemingford?)	½a. 1 r.	w. + o.	2s.
30.	Somersham	300 a.	(purpresture?)	

TABLE B

HUNTINGDONSHIRE ASSARTS IN MID THIRTEENTH CENTURY

(E32/40: 39 H III)

Entry No.	*Place*	*Acreage*
1.	Coppingford	3 r.
2.	Sibethorp (Ellington)	½r.
3.	Hocinton (Houghton?)	4 a.
4.	Raveley	3 a.
5.	(Agden: Great Staughton)	30 a.

TABLE C

ASSARTS IN ROYAL FORESTS OF HUNTINGDONSHIRE, 1 july, 1286

(E32/44)

Entry No.	*Place*	*Acreage*	*Crops*	*Value*
1.	Folksworth	2 a.	8 w. + 8 o.	24s.
2.	Walton	4 a.	8 w. + 8 o.	48s.
3.	Coppingford	1 r.	o. + f.	1d. ob.
4.	Stilton	2 a.	8 w. + 8 o.	24s.
5.	Winwick	1 a.	8 w. + 8 o.	12s.
6.	Folksworth	½r.	6 w. + 7 o.	13d.
7.	Perry	4 a.	6 w. + 7 o. + (1½a.) w.	39s. 6d.
	Perry	10 a.	6 w. + 7 o.	£4. 5s.
8.	Sawtry	2 a.	6 w. + 7 o.	36s.
	Sawtry	1 a.	w. + 3 o.	2s. 6d.
9.	Kingsdelf (Farcet)	35 a.	f. (meadow)	18s. 8d.
10.	Fletton	5ft x 20 p.		
11.	Folksworth	3 a.	6 w. + 10 o.	33s.
12.	Raveley	2 a.	6 w. + 10 o.	24s.
13.	Walton	5 a.	frisc'	

TABLE C cont'd

14.	Coppingford	½ a.	nil	
15.	Upton	2 a. ½ r.	6 w. + 10 o.	25s. 6d.
16.	Alconbury (Weston)	2½ a.	6 w. + 10 o.	30s.
17.	Easton	4 a.	6 w. + 10 o.	18s.
18.	Lymage	60 a.	(16 a.) o.	8s.
19.	Sibethorp (Ellington)	1 a.	6 w. + 10 o.	12s.
20.	Upton	½ r.	6 w. + 10 o.	9d.

NOTE: In the same manuscript is a list of assart privileges cited as

Charters of Hunts

a. Templars — general
b. Bishop of Ely — general; but gives names of his woods
c. Priory of Hunts
d. Abbot of Sawtry — general; 10 a. of assarts next fields of Suthwick and woods of Toten Ho and Sohil
e. Bishop of Ely — 186 acres in Hodestoke + 246½ in Litelbury + 520 a. 1 r. in Somersham
f. Canons of Merton — 50 a. in Alconbury
g. Vill of Hunts — general
h. Kimbolton — general
i. Warden — very detailed in Midelho, etc. — but no acreage
j. Simon s. of Richard — general

APPENDIX VII

EARLY THIRTEENTH-CENTURY ASSARTS IN LEICESTERSHIRE AND RUTLAND

The great range of assarting in the Rockingham Forest area in the early thirteenth century is further extended by the Forest Proceedings for Leicestershire and Rutland. Upon membrane 30 of E32/249 is a Regard taken at Oakham in 10 John. The entries are given below in the order of their appearance in the manuscripts. Most of the villages in the high ground of east Leicestershire are represented, as well as Rutland villages along the north-west bank of the Welland and up along west Rutland beyond Oakham. While the names of the tenants are not given here, it may be noted that for the Regards of Leicestershire 'the men' of Horninghold, Cranoe, Skeffington and Stanton are held responsible for the assarts.

FOUND SOWN IN THE FIRST REGARD FOR LEICESTERSHIRE

PLACE	*ASSART ACREAGE*	*CROP SOWN*
Horninghold	16 a. 1 r.	3 a. w.
		13 a. 1 r. o.
Cranoe	5 a.	w.
	1½ a.	w.
Goadby	6 a.	3 a. w.
		3 a. o.
Hallaton	3 a.	w.
Stanton	1 a.	w.
Keythorpe Hall	½ a.	o.
Skeffington	4 a.	w.
Skeffington	1 r.	w.
Tilton	2½ a.	w.
Launde Abbey	120 a.	60 a. w.
		60 a. o.
Withcote	4 a.	w.
Stanton	5 a.	w.

APPENDIX VII cont'd

FOUND SOWN IN THE SECOND REGARD

Horninghold	16 a. 1 r.	o.
Cranoe	5 a.	w.
Cranoe	1 a.	w.
Goadby	6 a.	o.
Stanton	2 a.	w.
Stanton	3 a.	w.
Stanton	5 a.	w.
Skeffington	4 a.	w.
Skeffington	1 r.	w.
Launde Abbey & Loddington	50 a.	1 a. w. 49 a. o.

NEW ASSARTS

Stanton	14 a.	13 a. w. 1 a. o.
Knossington	3 r.	w.
Withcote	4 a.	o.
Skeffington	1 a.	w.
Holy Oaks (Great Easton)	3 a. 1 r.	o.
Owston	2 a. 3 r.	o.
Owston	1 a. 1 r.	o.

FOUND SOWN IN THE FIRST REGARD OF RUTLAND

PLACE	*ASSART ACREAGE*	*CROP SOWN*
Ketton	½ a.	o.
Barrowden	2 a.	w.
Lyndon	10 a.	o.
Seaton	6 a.	o.
Liddington	27 a.	w.
Uppingham	40 a.	o.
Braunston	16 a.	3 a. w. 13 a. o.
Wardley	2 a.	o.
Wardley	3 a.	o.
Leighfield	½ a.	w.
Oakham	40 a.	o.
Martinsthorpe	6 a.	o.
Martinsthorpe	1 a.	o.

MANUSCRIPTS USED ARRANGED IN CHRONOLOGICAL ORDER

Note: See Introductory Notes to Appendices for detailed explanation of reasons for selecting these manuscripts.

NORTHAMPTONSHIRE

Salcey & Whittlewood:

E32/248
E32/249, m. 6 & 13
E32/64
E32/66
E32/69
E32/72
E32/76
E32/77
E32/101
E32/108
E32/115

Rockingham:

E32/249 m. 11 & 13
E32/67
E32/49, m. 28
E32/68
E32/73
E32/74
E32/85
E32/101
E32/100
E32/106
E32/110

BUCKINGHAMSHIRE

E32/249, m. 18 — 20
E32/2, m. 10

HUNTINGDONSHIRE

E32/248
E32/40
E32/44

LEICESTERSHIRE & RUTLAND

E32/249, m. 30

*INDEX OF PLACES**

BEDFORDSHIRE

Ampthill, 28, 56, 79
Arlesey, 28, 56, 80
Aspley Guise, 28, 55, 79, 92
Astwick, 28

Barton-in-the-Clay, 29
Beeston, 29, 56
Biggleswade, 28, 79
Bletsoe, 28, 56, 79, 92
Blunham, 28, 56
Brogborough, 28, 56, 79
Bromham, 27, 56

Cainhoe, 27, 55, 79, 92
Campton, 28, 55, 79
Cardington, 27, 55, 79, 92
Chanston, 27, 55, 92
Chellington, 19, 27
Cople, 28, 56
Cotes, 27, 56, 79, 92

Dilwick, 27, 55, 80
Dunton, 29, 55, 79

Eaton, 28, 55, 79, 87, 92
Edworth, 28
Eyworth, 27, 56, 80

Flitton, 29, 56
Flitwick, 28, 55, 79

Greathampstede, 28, 79, 92

Harrold, 29, 56, 80, 92
Haynes, 28, 56, 79
Henlow, 29, 56, 80
Higham Gobion, 28, 55, 79, 92
Hockliffe, 29, 56
Houghton, 28, 55, 79, 92
Hyde, La, 28

Kempston, 27, 55, 79, 92
Kempston Hardwick, 29
Keysoe, 27, 55, 79, 92

Langford, 29, 56, 80
Luton, 29, 55 (2), 80, 92

Meppershall, 28, 56, 80, 92
Millbrook, 27, 56, 79
Milton Ernest, 29, 56
Moggerhanger, 27, 55, 79, 92

Nares Gladly, 29
Northill, 28, 56, 79, 92

Odell, 29, 55
Odell, Little, 29, 55, 79

Podington, 29, 56, 80, 92

Radwell, 27, 56
Ravensden, 28, 55
Renhale, 27, 55, 79, 92
Risely, 19, 27

Sandy, 28, 55
Santon Barn, 29, 56, 80, 92
Shelton, 28, 92
Shillington, 29, 56, 92
Stagsden, 27, 56, 79, 92
Stanbridge, 20, 28, 55

* Bracketed place names throughout the volume, employed to indicate the main village or manor in the complex, or some such attribution to assist in identification, are not repeated in this index.

Staploe, 28, 92
Stevington, 27, 56, 80, 92
Stotfold, 28, 56, 79
Streatley, 28, 55, 92
Sudbury, 29, 56, 80, 92
Sundon, 29, 56, 80
Sutton, 28, 56, 79, 80

Tempsford, 28, 55
Thurleigh, 28, 56, 79
Toddington, 29, 56, 80
Turvey, 29, 56, 80

Warden, 27, 55, 79, 92
Westoning, 28, 55, 79, 92
Wilden, 27, 56, 80, 92
Wilden & Bolnhurst, 27
Willington, 28, 56, 79, 92
Wood Croft, 29, 55, 80 (2)
Woodhill, 55
Wootton, 28, 55, 79, 92
Wootton Pillinge, 28, 55, 79, 92
Wreste Park, 27, 56, 79
Wrestlingworth, 27, 56
Wyboston, 28, 56, 79
Wymington, 19, 27 (2), 55, 79

Yelden, 28, 56, 79

BUCKINGHAMSHIRE

Abinton, 139
Addington, 31, 59
Adstock, 31, 59
Akeley, 140, 142 (3), 143, 144 (2), 149 (2)
Amersham, 31, 58
Ashendon, 33
Aston Bernard, 33, 60, 82
Aston Clinton, 30
Aston Sanford, 33, 60
Astwood, 32, 81
Aylesbury, 30, 58, 81

Beachendon, 33, 60
Bernwood, 147, 150 (7)
Boarstall, 32
Bradenham, 33, 60
Brickhill, Great, 31, 58
Brickhill, Little, 31, 58, 93
Broughton, 32, 58
Broughton, Little, 32, 58, 81
Buckingham, 32, 59
Buckland, 30, 57, 81
Bunsty, 138
Burnham, 30, 57, 80, 93
Burnham & Eton, 30, 57, 80

Cadinton, 145
Caldecote, 33
Caldecote & Willen, 33, 60
Calverton, 33, 60, 82
Chalfont, 32, 93
Chalfont St. Giles, 31, 57, 80
Chearsley, 31, 58, 81
Cheddington, 32
Chelmscott, 57, 81
Chenies, 33, 60, 82, 93
Chesham, 29, 58
Chesham Bois, 29, 57, 80, 93
Chilton, 33, 59, 93
Chivery in Aston Clinton, 33, 60
Cippenham, 34, 59, 93
Cowley, 33, 60
Crafton, 30, 58, 81
Cublington, 20, 30, 57, 81

Dadford, 140, 142 (2)
Datchet, 20, 29, 57
Dinton, 33, 59, 93
Doddford, 144 (2)
Dorney, 32, 59, 81, 93
Dorton, 33, 60
Drayton Beauchamp, 32, 58
Drayton Parslow, 32, 58
Dunton, 32, 58, 81

Eakley Lanes, 32
Easington, 31, 60, 82
East Claydon, 34, 59, 81, 93
Edlesborough, 20, 30, 57, 80, 93
Ellesborough, 32, 58
Emberton, 31, 59, 93
Eton, 32, 59, 82

Evershaw in Biddlesden, 140, 142, 144
Eythorpe, 32, 59, 82
Eythorpe & Cranwell, 32

Farnham, 59, 93
Farnham Royal, 31
Feldham, 32, 58
Foscott, 93, 146, 148
Foscott, Great & Little, 33, 60
Fulbrook, 30, 57, 81
Fulmer, 32, 57

Gayhurst, 31, 59, 141, 144
Grendon Underwood, 30, 58, 81
Grove, 30, 57

Habinton, 142
Hambleden, 30, 58, 81, 93
Hampden, 32
Hanslope, 31, 58, 81, 93, 140 (17), 141 (6), 142 (9), 143 (21), 144, 145 (19), 146 (3)
Hardmead, 33, 60, 93
Hardwick, 20, 30, 58, 81
Hartwell, 32, 58, 81
Haversham, 30, 57, 93, 140, 141, 144
Hillesden, 32, 57, 81
Hitcham, 30, 57, 80, 93
Hitcham & Losmere, 57, 93
Hoggeston, 33, 60
Holmer Green, 31, 59, 93
Horton, 145
Horwood, Great & Little, 33, 60
Hoteleys, 139, 141 (2), 142, 143, 144

Ickford, 32, 59
Ilmer, 31, 59
Iver, 31, 59, 81

Kimble, Great & Little, 33, 60, 82
Kingsey, 32, 58, 81

La Burrow & Parmoor, 33, 59
La Waterhall, 32, 59, 82
Lathbury, 34, 59, 81, 140 (3), 141 (4), 143 (3), 144
Lavendon, 33, 59, 139 (3), 140 (4), 142 (2), 143, 144 (3)
Leckhampstead, 30, 57, 142 (2), 143 (2), 144, 146 (2), 148
Leckhampstead, Great, 30, 57, 93
Lillingstone, 142 (2), 143, 144 (2), 146 (9), 149 (7)
Linford, 30, 57
Linford, Great, 30, 57, 140, 143
Linford, Little, 30, 57, 80, 93
Linslade, 32, 93
Linslade & Southcott, 32, 57, 93
Losmere, 30, 57, 80, 93

Marlow, 31, 59, 82
Marlow, Great, 31, 59, 82
Marsworth, 31, 59, 81
Medenham, 29, 57, 80, 93
Milton Keynes, 34, 60
Missenden, 58, 93
Missenden, Great, 30, 58, 81, 93
Missenden, Little, 30, 58, 93
Moreton, 146, 149
Moulsoe, 57

Newport Pagnell, 30, 57, 80
Northall, 33, 60

Oak End, 33
Oakley, 32
Olney, 32, 59, 140 (2), 142, 144

Padbury, 31, 57, 80, 143 (2)
Penn, 33, 60, 93
Pirney, 32, 57
Pitstone, 32, 81, 93
Preston, 60, 82, 93
Preston Bissett, 33, 60

Quainton, 57

Ravenstone, 139 (12), 141 (11), 142 (6), 144 (13)
Risborough, 30, 57

Salden, 34, 60, 93
Saunderton, 32, 59
Seabrook, 20, 32, 58, 81

Shabbington, 30, 57, 81, 93
Shenley, 33, 93
Sherington, 31, 58, 81
Simpson, 60, 82, 93
Singleborough, 33, 60
Snelson, 32, 59
Stanton, 60
Stantonbury, 33, 60, 82, 93
Stewkley, 31, 59, 81, 93
Stoke, 145
Stoke Goldington, 31, 59, 81, 93, 140, 141 (2), 144 (2)
Stoke Halling, 59
Stoke Hammond, 32, 59
Stoke Poges, 20, 31, 59, 81
Stoking Green, 140, 141, 143 (2), 144

Thornton, 57
Tyringham, 32, 57, 81

Waddesdon, 32, 58
Wavendon, 30, 57, 93
Weedon, 34, 58, 81
Wendover, 31, 58
Wendover & Weston Turville, 31, 58, 81
Westbury, 140, 149
Westbury & Radclive, 33, 60
Weston, 20, 139 (7), 142 (6)
Weston Turville, 31 (2), 59
Weston Underwood, 141 (8), 142, 144 (4)
Whaddon, 33, 60
Whelpley Hill, 33, 59
Whitchurch, 29, 57, 80
Wing, 32
Wingrave, 32, 59
Woburn, 32, 59, 93
Wolverton, 34, 60, 82
Woodham, 58
Woolstone, 33, 60
Workington, 59, 82
Worminghall, 33, 59, 82
Woughton-on-the-Green, 33
Wycombe, 30, 57, 81, 93

HERTFORDSHIRE

Abbots & Kings Langley, 35
Albury, 34, 61, 82, 94
Almshoe, 36, 95
Anstey, 35
Anstey, Great, 35, 62, 83
Anstey, Little, 35, 62, 83
Aston, 62

Barwythe, 36
Batchwood, 35
Bayford, 36, 62, 83, 95
Bengeo, 36, 62, 83
Bennington, 36, 62, 95
Berkhamsted, 61, 82, 94
Berkhamsted, Great, 34
Berkhamsted, Little, 34, 61, 82, 94
Berwick, 35, 62, 83
Betlow, 36, 61, 83
Bishey Wood, 35, 62, 83
Bishey Wood, Great, 35, 62, 95
Bishops Hatfield, 35, 62, 83, 95
Broxbourne, 36, 61, 82
Buckland, 37, 62, 95

Chelsing, 36, 61, 94
Cheshunt, 36, 62, 84
Cottered, 36

Eastwick, 35, 61, 95
Eastwick atte Flore, 35, 61, 83, 94
Essendon, 36, 62, 83

Flamstead, 34, 61, 82, 94
Furneux Pelham, 36, 61, 83, 94

Gaddesden, 35, 61, 83, 94
Gaddesden, Great, 35, 61, 83
Gaddesden, Little, 35

Harpsfield Hall, 37
Hatfield, 83
Hatherfeld, 37
Hemel Hempstead, 35, 61, 82, 94
Hertingfordbury, 35, 62, 83, 95

Hitchin, 35, 61, 82
Hoddesdon, 36, 62, 83, 95
Holwell, 36, 62, 83
Holwell, Little, 36, 62, 83, 95
Hormead, 35, 61, 83, 94
Hormead, Little, 35, 61, 83
Hunsdon, 35, 60, 82, 94

Kings Langley, 62, 95
King's Walden, 35, 61, 83
Knebworth, 36, 62, 84, 95

Lilley, 36, 95

Mardleybury, 37, 62, 84, 95
Marlin Farm, 36, 61, 94
Meesden, 34, 61, 94
Minsden, 36
Munden, Great & Little, 36, 83, 94

Nuthampstead, 36, 62, 84

Offley, 34, 82, 94

Patmore Hall, 36, 61, 83, 94
Pirton, 35, 61, 83, 94
Pishobury, 61, 82, 94
Plessis, 37, 62, 84, 95
Pope's Hall, 35, 61, 83, 94

Rableyheath, 35, 61
Redbourn, 36, 62
Reden, 62
Reed, 35, 62, 83

Sacombe, 34, 60, 82, 94
Sawbridgeworth, 20, 34, 61, 82, 88, 94
Shenley, 35, 83
Stagenhoe, 35, 62
Standon, 34, 61, 82, 94
Stanstead Abbots, 62
Stapleford, 61
Stevenage, 36
Stocks, 36, 94
Studham, 36, 62

Thele, 36, 62, 83, 95
Theobald St., 35, 61, 83, 94
Therfield, 37, 62, 84
Thorley, 36, 61, 83, 94
Throcking, 35
Thundridge, 61, 83, 94
Twendesbury, 36, 62, 83, 95

Walden, Kings & St. Pauls, 94
Walhamstede, 36, 62, 95
Walkern, 34, 61, 94
Walterend Farm, 36, 62
Ware, 36, 61, 83
Watton at Stone, 35, 61, 83, 94
Welles, 37, 62, 84
Weston, 36, 62
Weston by Baldock, 36
Westreed, 35, 83
Westwick Hall, 36, 62, 95
Wigginton, 35, 61, 83
Willian, 35, 83
Wyddial, 34, 61, 83
Wymondley, Great, 34, 61, 83
Wymondley, Little, 34, 94

HUNTINGDONSHIRE

Abbots Ripton, 152 (2)
Agden, 152
Alconbury, 151 (2), 153n, 153
Alconbury & Weston, 37, 63, 95, 153

Botolph Bridge, 37, 63
Botolph Bridge & Orton, 37, 63
Boughton, 37, 63
Brampton, 37, 63, 84, 95
Buckden, 151

Caldecote, 37, 63, 84, 96
Catworth, 38, 63
Chesterton, 38
Colne, 38, 63
Conington, 38, 63
Coppingford, 152 (3), 153

Denton, 38, 63
Diddington, 20, 38, 63, 95
Dillington, 37, 62, 84, 95, 151 (2)

Easton, 151, 153
Ellington, 151 (3)
Ellington Thorpe, 37, 63, 84, 95
Everton (Beds), 37, 63, 84, 95
Eynesbury, 38

Fen Stanton & Hilton, 37, 63, 84
Fletton, 152
Folksworth, 38, 64, 152 (3)

Gidding, Great, 37, 62
Glatton, 37, 63, 96
Grafham, 38, 95, 151
Gransden, Great, 38, 63, 96

Hail Weston, 151
Hamerton, 37, 63, 84, 95
Hemingford, 37, 63, 96, 152
Hemingford Grey, 37, 63, 84
Hocinton, 152
Hodestoke, 153n.
Honour of Hunts, 151 (2)
Hunts, vill of, 153n.

Kimbolton, 20, 38, 63, 153n.
Kingsdelf, 151, 152

Litelbury, 153n.
Lymage, 38, 63, 84, 95, 151, 153

Offord Cluny, 38
Offord Darcy, 38, 63, 84
Orton Longueville, 37, 63

Paxton, Little, 37, 63, 84
Paxton, Great, 38, 63
Perry, 37, 151 (3), 152 (2)
Pidley, 38, 64

Raveley, 152 (2)

Sawtry, 63, 152 (3)
Sibethorp, 152, 153
Somersham, 151, 152, 153n.
Southoe, 37, 63, 84, 95
Southoe & Boughton, 37, 63
Southoe Luvetot, 37, 63
Southoe & Orton Waterville, 37, 63, 95
Staughton, Great, 38, 63, 84, 95
Stilton, 152
St. Neots, 38, 63
Stukeley, 151, 152 (2)
Stukeley, Great, 38, 63

Toseland, 38, 63, 84, 96
Turberville, 37, 63, 96

Upton, 38, 84, 95, 152, 153 (2)
Upwood, 38, 63

Walton, 152 (3)
Warden, 153n.
Washingley, 20, 38, 63, 84, 95, 152 (3)
Weston, 63
Winwick, 152

Yelling, 37, 63, 96

LEICESTERSHIRE

Ab Kettleby, 39, 64, 84
Arnesby, 65
Ashby Folville, 39, 64
Ashby Town, 40
Ashby de la Zouch, 21, 38, 64
Aythelaxton, 39

Baggrave, 39
Barkestone, 38, 65, 84
Barrow-upon-Soar, 39, 64, 84, 96
Barwell, 38, 65
Beaumanor, 39, 64
Bitteswell, 40
Blaston, 39
Bosworth, 40, 65
Bottesford, 20, 21, 38, 64
Branston, 21, 38, 64
Bringhurst, 39, 64, 65

Broughton, 39
Buckminster, 39
Burbage, 38, 65
Burton, 40, 65
Burton Overy, 39, 64
Burton on the Wolds, 40, 65

Castle Donington, 40, 65, 84
Church Langton, 40
Claxton, 64
Claybrook, Great & Little, 21, 38
Congerstone in Shakerstone, 40, 65
Cotesbach, 39, 64, 84
Cotes de Val, 40
Cotestown, 39
Cranoe, 154 (2), 155 (2)
Croxton, 39, 64, 84
Croxton, South, 39

Dalby Great, 40, 65
Desford, 21, 38, 64
Diseworth, 40, 65
Donington, 20, 39, 65, 84
Drayton, 39, 64

Earl Shilton, 21, 38, 64
Easton, Great, 39, 64
Evington, 21, 38, 64, 84

Foston, 20, 38, 64, 84
Freeby, 40, 65

Gale Orton, 40, 65
Goadby, 154, 155
Groby, 21, 38, 64
Gumley, 40, 65

Haleweton, 64
Hallaton, 40, 154
Hemington, 40
Hinckley, 21, 38
Holy Oaks, 64, 155
Horninghold, 154 (2), 155
Hose, 65
Houghton-on-the-Hill, 39, 64
Hugglescote, 65

Kegworth, 40, 65
Keythorpe, 40
Keythorpe Hall, 154
Kirby Ballards, 38, 64, 96
Kirkby Mallory, 39, 64
Knaptoft, 39, 64
Knossington, 155

Launde Abbey, 154, 155
Leicester, 39, 64
Lobthorpe (Lincs), 39, 64, 84, 96
Long Whatton, 65
Loughborough, 65
Lowesby, 21, 38, 64
Lutterworth, 39, 64

Marefield South, 39
Medbourne, 39, 84
Melton Mowbray, 40, 65
Mountsorrel, 84
Mowsley, 21, 39, 65
Muston, 39, 65

Nailstone, 39, 65
Narborough, 39, 64
Neville Holt, 40, 65
Newbold Saucey, 21, 39
Newton Harcourt, 40, 65, 84
Normanton, 20, 39, 64

Odstone, 40, 65
Overton, 40
Owston, 155 (2)

Pickwell, 20, 39, 64
Prestwold, 40, 65

Quartemars, 40
Quenby, 39

Redmile, 39, 64

Saddington, 20, 21, 38, 64
Saltby, 39
Saxby, 39, 65
Scheyle, 39

Seagrave, 40, 65, 84
Skeffington, 154 (3), 155 (3)
Somerby, 39
Stanton, 154 (3), 155 (4)

Thorton, 39, 65
Thorpe Arnold, 64
Thrussington, 40, 65
Tilton, 154
Twyford, 39, 64

Upton, 39, 64

Welland, 154
Whetstone, 39, 64
Whitwick, 65
Willoughby Waterless, 39, 64, 84
Withcote, 154, 155
Witherley, 39
Wymeswold, 38, 65

NORTHAMPTONSHIRE

Abington, 42, 69
Abthorpe, 102, 103, 108, 112, 122
Alderton, 43, 68, 85, 103, 113, 121 (5), 129
Aldwinkle, 115, 125, 126, 130
Alecote, 129
Almer, 70
Alneston, 45
Anderman, 108
Apethorpe, 104, 126, 127
Ashley, 43, 70
Ashton, 43, 67, 111, 120 (3)
Astcote, 44
Astwell, 44, 70, 108, 112, 122

Barne, 123 (2)
Barnwell, 41, 68
Barton Seagrave, 44, 70
Benefield, 43, 103, 115, 125, 126 (2), 129
Berford, 130
Bickenho, 122 (2)
Billing, 20, 43
Billing, Great, 44, 70
Blakesley, 112, 114
Blatherwycke, 40, 67, 116, 126, 127, 130
Blisworth, 111, 114
Bozeat, 45, 71
Bradden, 45, 71
Brampton Ash, 44, 70, 124 (9)
Braunston, 42, 70
Braybrooke, 42, 68, 114
Brgde, 123
Brigstock, 104, 114
Brixsworth, 44, 70
Broughton, 44, 70
Brugbrook, 43
Bucknell Wood, 44, 70, 122
Bulwick, 43, 67, 116, 126 (4)
Burcote, 103, 104
Burgwode, 124
Burnewode, 120 (2), 128, 133
Burton Latimer, 42, 69, 85
Byfield, 43, 67

Castor, 70, 117
Castle Ashby, 41, 68, 85, 96
Chalcombe, 44, 70
Chelveston-cum-Caldecott, 45, 71
Chester Ho, 45, 70
Chipping Warden, 42, 68
Cliffe Forest, 128, 131
Cogenhoe, 45, 71, 102 (2)
Cokefield, 130
Colershawe, 114
Corby, 41, 68, 85, 104, 114, 124 (2)
Cosgrove, 45, 71, 86, 96, 103, 113
Cosgrove & Furtho, 45, 71, 96
Cosgrove & Puxley, 45, 71, 96
Cotsm, 117
Cotterstock, 20, 41, 85, 115
Cottingham, 124, 125, 129
Cotton, 43, 68, 116
Courteenhall, 102 (2), 111
Cransley, Great, 45
Creaton, 44
Crick, 42, 69
Croughton, 43, 67
Crowland, 104

Culworth, 42, 69

Dallington, 41, 68
Deanshanger, 45, 71, 86, 129
Deene, 116, 125 (3), 129
Deenethorpe, 106, 116, 125, 129
Denford, 44, 70
Desborough, 43, 114, 124, 129
Dingley, 124, 129
Doddington, Great, 40, 96
Dodford, 43, 68
Drayton, 43, 68, 85
Duddington, 102, 104 (3), 115, 126 (4)
Duston, 42, 70, 85, 102, 112

Earls Barton, 44, 70
East Carlton, 41, 68, 96, 114, 125
East Farndon, 43
East Haddon, 42, 85
Easton-on-the-Hill, 20, 41, 67, 85, 116, 120
Easton Neston, 120, 129
Eastwell, 108
Ecton, 20, 44, 69
Evenley, 42, 69, 85

Falcutt, 44
Falshelm, 117
Farndon, 68
Farthinghoe, 45
Fawsley, 45, 71
Faxton, 41, 67, 85, 96, 106, 119 (2), 124 (2), 127
Finedon, 42, 69, 85
Fotheringhay, 43, 68, 85, 127
Furtho, 113

Gayton, 44
Geddington, 106, 114
Glapthorn, 43, 104 (2), 115, 126
Grafton, 43, 70, 96, 103, 106 (2), 107 (3), 108 (2), 121 (5)
Grafton Regis, 113, 128
Grafton Underwood, 125
Greatworth, 43, 69
Green's Norton, 121 (3), 122 (7), 129
Grendon, 44, 70, 86
Gretton, 43, 67, 70, 85, 104, 106, 116, 125, 126, 127

Hackleton, 129
Hale, 116, 127 (3)
Halefield Lodge, 42, 69
Halse, 20, 44, 69
Halwton, 117
Hardwick, 45, 71
Harpole, 44, 70, 112
Harringworth, 41, 67, 85, 116
Harrowden, Great, 45, 71
Hartwell, 108, 111
Harwell, 111, 127
Haselbech, 44, 70
Helmdon, 108, 113
Helpston, 116
Henwick, 116
Higham Ferrers, 42, 69, 85
Hoggenhul, 122
Horton, 43, 102 (2), 103, 106, 111, 114, 120 (11), 128, 133
Houghton, Great, 41, 68, 85
Houghton, Little, 42, 68
Hulcote, 111

Irchester, 45, 71, 86
Irthingborough, 71
Islip, 41, 68

Kelmarsh, 45, 71
King's Cliffe, 104 (2), 115, 126
Kings Sutton, 45, 71, 86
Kislingbury, 45, 70
Kingshill, 129
Kirby Hall, 116

Laxton, 116, 127, 130
Lilford-cum-Wigsthorpe, 44, 70, 86
Linsdon, 129
Linton, fee of, 123
Litleley, 122
Loddington, 43, 70, 86

Long Buckby, 20, 44, 70
Lowick, 43, 114, 115, 125
Lyveden, 125

Mears Ashby, 41, 68, 85, 96
Milton, 42, 70, 96
Moor End, 44, 70
Moreton Pinkney, 44, 70
Moulton, 44, 70, 86

Naseby, 41, 67, 85
Nassington, 104, 110, 115
Nassington & Yarwell, 43, 68
Newbottle, 20, 40, 67, 124
Newton, 114, 125 (2)
Northampton, 44, 69
Northawe, 127, 130
Norton, 45, 70, 86, 96, 103

Oakley, 114
Oakley, Great, 41, 68, 106, 114, 125 (2), 127, 129
Oakley, Little, 41, 68, 85, 96, 114, 125, 130
Old & New Lyveden, 115
Ospery, 123, 129
Oundle, 45

Passenham, 41, 68, 85, 96, 133
Paston, 117
Pattishall, 42, 69, 85
Paulerspury, 112, 121 (8)
Pery, 69, 85, 108 (2)
Peterborough, Soke of, 104, 105, 110
Piddington, 107, 108 (4), 112, 120, 133
Pilton, 20, 43, 115, 125, 129, 143
Plumpton, 41, 68, 85, 107
Plumpton End, 113, 121 (2)
Potterspury, 42, 69, 85
Preston Deanery, 112, 133
Preston Wood, 44, 70
Puxley, 41, 123 (2), 128
Pytchley, 44, 70

Quinton, 44, 70, 120 (2)

Radstone, 43, 67
Raunds, 42, 69, 85
Rising Bridge, 116, 130
Roade, 102, 108, 111
Rockingham Forest, 43, 68, 96, 103, 104 (2), 105 (3), 106, 107 (2)n, 109 (2), 110 (2), 116, 118 (2), 119, 128 (2), 131 (3), 156
Rohawe & Essawe, 114
Rothersthorpe, 112
Rothwell, 43, 67, 85, 96, 114
Rushton, 42, 69, 102, 103, 106 (2), 114 (2), 124 (2), 127 (2), 129

Salcey, 102 (2), 103, 104 (2), 105, 106 (5), 109, 110, 111, 118, 119, 128 (3), 131 (4), 132, 138 (2), 156
Scaldwell, 44
Scrob Passenham, 123
Seawell Farm, 44
Shaw, 111
Shutlanger, 111
Sibberton, 127 (2)
Silverstone, 43, 68, 104 (2), 108, 113-114, 122 (6), 123 (10), 128, 130, 133
Slapton, 41, 68
Slipton, 114
Southorpe, 117
Southwick, 44, 115, 126, 127 (3)
Stanion, 114, 125, 130
Steane, 45, 69
Stodinton, 117
Stoke Albany, 42, 69, 85
Stoke Bruerne, 43, 68, 111, 112, 129
Stoke Doyle, 102, 115, 125, 126, 127
Stoke Park, 112
Stoke & Wilbarston, 71, 86
Stokes, 108 (2)
Stowe, 45, 70
Stowe Nine Churches, 112
Stratford, 68
Suardshawe, 126

Sub Piri, 116
Sudborough, 114, 125, 126, 129
Sulgrave, 42, 69, 86
Sweteleye, 123 (2)

Thornhawe, 130
Thorpbelet, 124
Thorpe, 42, 69, 85, 104
Thorpe Mandeville, 45, 71
Tiffield, 129
Titchmarsh, 41, 68, 85
Torpel, 20, 41, 85
Torpel Ufford, 44, 67, 70
Towcester, 43, 70, 86, 102, 103, 108, 113

Ufford, 116
Upton, 41, 68, 85, 117

Wadenhoe, 40, 67, 85, 115, 125 (2)
Wakerley, 42, 69, 85, 96, 116
Walton, 41, 68, 85, 117 (2)
Walyle, 127
Wappenham, 69, 85
Wasseneye, 128
Watford, 43, 70
Weedon Beck, 102, 103, 108, 112
Weedon Lois, 43, 69, 85
Weekley, 43, 68, 106, 125
Weldon, 41
Weldon, Great, 116, 125 (2), 129
Weldon, Little, 20, 42, 69, 96, 106, 116, 125 (2), 127 (4), 129
Welford, 44, 69
Weston, 42, 69, 85, 126
Weston Pynkney, 42
Westpery, 41, 68, 85, 96, 103, 121 (9), 128, 143
West Wood, 117
Weton, 108
Whitfield, 43, 85
Whittlebury, 113
Whittlewood, 44, 103, 104, 105, 106 (4), 109, 110, 118, 119, 128 (3), 131 (4), 132, 138 (2), 156
Wicken, 20, 41, 67, 113, 123 (5), 128
Wike, 43, 68
Wilby, 44, 96
Wollaston, 45, 71
Wood Burcote, 113
Woodcroft Castle, 116
Woodnewton, 127
Wootton, 44, 70, 86, 112, 129
Wootton fee, 129
Wulfey, 111
Wyberdel, 124
Wychenmord, 117
Wytinge, 127, 130

Yardley, 107, 108, 121
Yardley Gobion, 42, 69, 85
Yarwell, 43, 68, 85, 115

NOTTINGHAMSHIRE

Arnold, 47, 67

Balderton, 20, 46, 66
Barnstone & Tithby, 47, 67
Barton in Fabis, 47, 67
Bothamsall, 46, 66
Bridgeford, 86
Brinsley, 47, 67
Bunny, 46, 86

Car Colston, 46
Carlton in Lindrick, 20, 46
Caunton, 47, 67
Clifton, 46, 86 (2)
Cossall, 45, 65
Cromwell, 46, 66
Cuckney, 46, 66

Eakring, 46, 66
Eaton, 46, 86
East Bridgeford, 46, 66
East & West Leake, 46, 86
Egmanton, 46, 86
Epperstone, 46, 66

Gameston, 46, 66
Gonalston, 46, 66
Granby, 47, 67
Grassthorpe, 47, 67
Grimston Hall, 47, 67
Gringley, 46
Grove, 46, 66

Hareston, 66
Harworth, 47, 67
Headon, 66
Hoveringham & Flinham, 66
Hucknall Torkard, 46, 67

Kingshaugh Ho, 46, 66
Kingston, 45
Kirkby, 46, 66
Kneesall, 46, 66

Lambley, 46, 66
Langar, 46, 66, 86
Laxton, 20, 47, 66
Leverton, North, 47, 67

Mansfield, 47
Markham Clinton, 45, 66
Marnham, 45, 66
Muskham, 66
Muskham, North, 47, 67

Nettleworth Manor, 46

Orston, 46, 66

Perlethorpe, 47, 67

Ratcliffe & Kingston, 45
Ratcliffe on Soar, 45, 66
Ratcliffe on Trent, 45, 86

Saxondale, 46
Scarthing Moor, 45
Scheggehagh, 45
Shelford, 66
Skegby, 45, 66
Stapleford, 46
Staythorpe, 45, 66
Staunton-in-the-Vale, 46, 86
Stoke Bardolph, 46, 66
Stoke, East, 46, 66
Strelley, 46, 66
Sutton, 46, 66

Thorney, 47, 67
Toton, 46, 66
Trowell, 47, 67
Tuxford, 46, 66

Wansley, 47, 67
Warsop, 46, 66
Weston, 46
Widmerpool, 46, 66
Wilford, 46
Wiverton Hall, 46, 47, 66
Wollaton, 45, 65
Worksop, 46, 66

RUTLAND

Ashwell, 47, 71, 86

Barrow, 47, 71
Barrowden, 17n, 47, 71, 86, 155
Braunston, 155

Casterton, 47, 86, 96
Casterton, Little, 47, 71

Egleton, 47
Empingham, 71
Essedine, 48, 72
Exton, 48, 72

Glaston, 48, 72
Greetham, 47, 71

Haliok, 47, 71

Ketton, 47, 71, 155

Langham, 20, 48, 72, 86
Leighfield, 155
Liddington, 155
Lyndon, 155

Market Overton, 20, 48, 72, 86
Martinsthorpe, 155 (2)

Oakham, 20, 47, 71, 86, 154 (2), 155

Preston & Uppingham, 47, 71, 86

Ryhall, 48, 72

Seaton, 48, 72, 155
Stoke Dry, 47, 71, 86, 96
Stretton, 47, 71

Upper Hambleton, 48, 72
Uppingham, 96, 155

Wardley, 155 (2)
Whissendene, 47, 71